Point
Reyes

PICTURE COURTESY OF POINT REYES NATIONAL SEASHORE

Gayle Baker, Ph.D.

Other books by Gayle Baker:
  The Wet Mountain Valley, 1975
  Trial and Triumph, 1977
  Catalina Island, 2002
  Santa Barbara, 2003
  Cambria, 2003
  Newport Beach, 2004
  Denver, 2004

Printed in USA by Vaughan Printing, Inc.

Library of Congress Cataloging in Publication Data:

Baker, Gayle
    Point Reyes/Gayle Baker, Ph.D.
    1st p. cm. ed.
    Includes index.
    ISBN 0-9710984-5-X
    History of Point Reyes Peninsula, Marin County, California
    I. Title

    PCN 2004103113

Cover by **Larry Iwerks,** *who studied at San Francisco State
University, Mendocino Art Center, and Santa Barbara Art Institute
under veteran landscape painter Ray Strong. Larry continues to
paint Western landscapes from his studio in Santa Barbara.*

Table of Contents

A Tribal Homeland 5

Explorers and Missionaries 11

Ranchos and Boundary Battles 21

Butter at Its Best 31

The Crumbling Shafter-Howard Empire 53

Lighthouse and Shipwrecks 63

New Owners 89

Connected to the Past; Eye to the Future 97

Index 109

Sources and Acknowledgments 111

Woman Standing in Crack Caused by 1906 Earthquake

A Tribal Homeland

Point Reyes, a stunning, weather-battered peninsula only an hour's drive from densely-populated San Francisco, is rich with compelling stories of its local tribes, tragic shipwrecks, wily lawyers, and dairying families who lived and loved there. The only National Seashore on the West Coast, it is also the site of the first English landing in North America. Bounded on its eastern edge by the towering Inverness Ridge, its far western tip, the Point Reyes Headland, rises 600 feet above the surf. Between the ridge and the point stretch miles of dense forests, lush wetlands, pristine beaches, and some of the richest grasslands in America.

This priceless cultural, scientific, and recreational area is a triangular peninsula that appears to be a temporarily attached appendage to the original coastline. And, that is exactly what it is. Once near Los Angeles, it has traveled north for millions of years. Between it and the rest of Marin County lies the invisible fissure in the earth well-known to us as the San Andreas Fault, a primary joint in the surface of the planet. Visible to the north as Tomales Bay and to the south as Bolinas Lagoon, this fault forms the eastern boundary of the Point Reyes Peninsula.

While most of California is on the North American Plate, Point Reyes rests on the Pacific Plate. These plates are mobile, with Point Reyes moving toward Canada at the geologically rapid pace of two inches per year. When stress caused by the interaction of these plates builds to a climax, California has another one of its earthquakes, and Point Reyes leaps northward. During the 1906 Earthquake, the entire peninsula sprang north 15 feet in 40 seconds.

Geologically unique, Point Reyes also differs from the rest of California in its weather, its stories, and its future. Known as the foggiest spot on the West Coast, it is the site of many of the nation's most extraordinary shipwrecks, while its fog-fed grasslands have nourished some of its finest dairy cows. Unique in its settlement patterns, it was more populated before the Spanish arrived than in subsequent centuries. Known as the "Island in Time," this magnificent peninsula—insulated, isolated, and protected—enjoys a history and a future far different from the densely-developed towns dominating much of coastal California.

Home of the Coast Miwoks

Point Reyes' first inhabitants, the Coast Miwok, have left evidence of well over a hundred encampments on the peninsula. Seasonal hunters and gatherers rather than cultivators, they were nourished by the fish, clams, mussels, and crab from its bountiful waters, in addition to the deer, elk, bear, mud hen, geese, and small game they hunted with either spears or bows and arrows. Although they did not cultivate the land, they were able use the plentiful acorns as a staple part of their diet by removing the tannic acid and making a pulp that was stored in dry granaries. Their peaceable and spiritual existence, rich with abundant food, lasted for centuries. They greeted the first explorers to reach the peninsula with friendliness and generosity, unaware that the arrival of the Spanish would dramatically change their lives.

Although the exact location of **Sir Francis Drake's** anchorage has provided four centuries of controversy, evidence has confirmed that he landed near some Coast Miwok settlements in 1579. Although his log has never been found, observations, presumably written by his chaplain, have provided valuable information. These observations described the genial welcome Drake and his men received. A chief and his retinue in ceremonial costumes, followed by unclothed men and women dressed in skins and bulrushes, exchanged gifts and greetings with Drake. Impressed by their hospitality, the chaplain observed:

> . . . a people of a tractable, free, and loving nature, without guile or treachery. [The men were] strong of body. . .

exceeding swift in running [and] skilled spearing fish in
shallow water [while the women were] very obedient to
their husbands, and exceedingly ready in all services; yet
of themselves offering to do nothing without the consents
or being called of the men.

After Drake and his men sailed away, the Coast Miwok returned to their peaceful routine. It was not until the late 18th century that their lives changed when the Spanish began building missions. Padres from the nearby Mission San Rafael journeyed to the peninsula to convert the Coast Miwok. They found over 50 villages with a population now estimated to be nearly 3000. While attempting to convert them, these padres disrupted their traditional way of life in addition to inadvertently introducing diseases that brought untimely deaths, fewer births, and significantly increased infant mortality rates.

By the 1830s, the missions had been replaced by the Mexican ranchos (ranches). Some surviving Coast Miwok journeyed inland to escape the looming civilization, while others labored on ranchos and, later, dairy ranches. Today, many of their grandchildren and great-grandchildren remain in the area, enriching their modern lives with the traditions of their ancestors.

The Kelly Interviews

For over a century, anthropologists from University of California, Berkeley have been accumulating data concerning the Coast Miwok. Early in the 1930s, a graduate student, **Isabel Kelly,** was assigned to interview 90-year old Tomas Comtechal, a respected singer, dancer, leader, and doctor. Kelly settled nearby for five months and wrote notes of these interviews that filled eight books. From these interviews, she learned of singers who could entice salmon from their hiding places in streams and women of power and influence. After her interview with Comtechal, she began interviewing Maria Copa Frias, a Miwok born just after the Civil War, and in less than two weeks, she had recorded over 100 more pages of notes.

These interviews provided a detailed picture of the daily lives of the Coast Miwok. Kelly learned that they were capable hunters and gatherers. They lived peacefully with neighbors in a temperate climate that abounded with food, including fish, shellfish, game, seeds, and two kinds of edible kelp. Hunting with bows, they used obsidian-tipped arrows kept in quivers made of animal skins. They also used slings for duck hunting. Highly spiritual, they often practiced sexual abstinence before hunting and fishing trips and carried charms of polished stone or chipped obsidian for luck.

The Coast Miwoks built both thatched and earth-covered semi-subterranean huts. Beds were made of rushes. The larger villages also had a variety of ceremonial huts, including the sweathouse, a subterranean chamber four to five feet deep covered by earth; social and work centers; dance huts; and the special hut for the young girls celebrating their first menstrual cycle.

Most men were semi-naked wearing only a deerskin loincloth, while women generally wore aprons of grass or fringed deer hide and capes woven out of small skins. Some pierced their ears, as they believed it contributed to longevity, while a few of the elderly had tattoos on their chests, drawn with a sharp bone and poison oak. Neither men nor women wore shoes. Men had beards and long hair that they bundled up, while women wore their long hair either braided or bundled. Adult males and some women, mostly the elderly ones, smoked tobacco in a pipe. They also smoked the hallucinogenic jimson weed.

The women were skilled basket weavers who coiled or twined baskets for special functions. Some baskets were utilitarian and watertight, while others were decorative, often adorned with feathers and shell beads. Men crafted tule canoes, propelled by a double-bladed wooden paddle, that they used to journey offshore to fish. They had a well-developed monetary system based on clamshell beads, with varying currencies represented by thin, thick, and extra thick beads. They often wore these beads as necklaces or hung them on baskets and staffs to display their wealth. During times of leisure, women enjoyed a game resembling dice, while men played hockey. Children's toys included jacks, clay, stick dolls, and string figures.

Larger villages had a leader who usually gave advice and spoke for them. According to Kelly, "He 'took care' of the people, offered advice, and harangued them daily, addressing them personally, not through a crier or orator." When it was time for a new chief, the tribe's elderly women and the old chief instructed the new leader, clear evidence that women played a powerful role in Coast Miwok society. In cases in which the old chief did not then abdicate, he was poisoned. In her interviews, Kelly also discovered that some older men sought liaisons with younger women and that these older men occasionally poisoned younger men so that they would not interfere with these liaisons.

Spiritual and Ceremonial Life

In addition to the details about their daily habits, these interviews provided a treasure trove of information about Coast Miwok beliefs and ceremonies. They worshipped natural forces and believed that the world had been created by the coyote and fire brought by the hummingbird. Most ceremonies were conducted by secret societies comprised of both men and women or women only. They were held to cure, poison, lay the dead to rest, and mark passages to adulthood. Spiritual leaders, either curers or poisoners, led these ceremonies. Participants painted their bodies and wore feathers as belts, head-dresses, and garments. Occasionally they also wore pelican skins with abalone buttons and shell disk beads. Music accompanied the ceremonies and was provided by log drums, split sticks, rattles, bone whistles, and elderberry flutes.

Although the Coast Miwok cremated their dead, archeological burial sites have also been discovered. Whether cremated or buried, a mourning ceremony was performed, and the deceased's name was not spoken until the memory of the death had faded. To mark the one-year anniversary of the death, another ceremony was conducted in which mourners danced, lamented, and participated in a ritual wash-ing. Personal property of the deceased was often destroyed, but was occasionally redistributed to other tribesmen.

The passage into adulthood for a young woman was ceremoniously observed at her first menstrual cycle. For four days, she was confined to a menstrual hut or isolated in her own hut. Her special deerskin bed was placed over a low fire, and she was not allowed to bathe. Her mother and grandmothers sang and danced while she used a scratching stick. After the four days, the young woman was freed from her confinement and could join feasting and dancing. During this dance and directly after it, she was sometimes tattooed and encouraged to have sexual relations.

The male initiation, called a ghost ceremony, prohibited women. For four days, boys were covered with black paint, held over the fire and occasionally tossed over it. They were only allowed to eat acorn soup and pinole and, like the young women, used sticks to scratch themselves. On the last night of the ceremony, the boys were thrown through the smoke hole in the roof.

Revival of Traditions

While information on most California tribes is limited to archeological discoveries, explorers' records, and mission documents, the work of University of California, Berkeley anthropologists and the in-depth interviews by Kelly have immeasurably enriched our understanding of the daily lives of the Coast Miwoks. These Berkeley scholars have spent a century providing a rich, multi-faceted glimpse of this fascinating group of Point Reyes inhabitants who flourished for centuries before the missionaries arrived.

In addition to this treasure trove of information, in 1992, Coast Miwok descendents established the Federated Indians of Graton Rancheria and, by 2001, had 400 members who could prove their descent from local tribes. Today, they enjoy the rebirth of traditional customs and ceremonies, often held in the National Seashore's re-created Coast Miwok village. Despite the tragic loss of their peaceful, self-sufficient way of life, our abundant information allows us to envision the tribes who lived, loved, worshipped, and died on this magnificent peninsula.

Explorers and Missionaries

Although most historians cite **Juan Rodriguez Cabrillo's** journey as California's most important early exploration, it is the landing of the English explorer, Sir Francis Drake, at Point Reyes that dominates discussion of this era. Significant as the first European landing in Northern California and the first English landing in North America, the location Drake selected has sparked countless hours of spirited debate spanning four centuries. Although the controversy still rages, most agree the evidence points toward Point Reyes' Drakes Bay as his refuge.

Despite the importance of Drake's landing in California, he was not the first European to claim Point Reyes. The first to sail by northern California was the 1542 expedition that had been led by Cabrillo, a Portuguese sailing under the Spanish flag. Although he died before reaching Point Reyes, the voyage continued north to Oregon under new command before returning to Mexico, its commander having claimed all of California for Spain. In addition to Cabrillo's ships, early Spanish trading galleons journeying between the Philippines and Acapulco often followed the California coast and passed near Point Reyes.

It was not these Spanish explorers, but Drake, who first landed in the area. In 1579, Drake sighted Point Reyes while sailing along the California coast looking for a safe harbor to make much-needed repairs to his weather-beaten ship, the *Golden Hinde* (named for a type of deer), before crossing the Pacific to return to England. A successful English privateer, his ship was heavily laden with treasure he had taken from the Spanish, loot he felt that he had earned honorably by following the accepted rules of plunder.

The oldest of 12, Drake was sent to sea as a boy. By his 20s he was in command of an English ship, *Judith*, in a small fleet charged with the task of breaking the Spanish monopoly in the New World. In

September 1568, storm damage forced him to bring *Judith* into a Mexican port. In accordance with rules of the sea, Drake negotiated the promise of a safe exit from the Spanish-controlled harbor when repairs had been completed. A mere two days later, this agreement was broken, and *Judith* was attacked. After a fierce defense, Drake and his crew escaped, but Drake never forgot. He sought restitution for this breach of faith by focusing his energy on stealing Spanish treasure. This reaction was reasonable for the times, as it was a well-established principle that compensation could be taken by force from a country that acted dishonorably.

Before he struck, Drake took several voyages of reconnaissance. His planning paid off handsomely, for he captured a mule train crossing the Isthmus of Panama heavily laden with gold from Peruvian mines. He returned to England wealthy and acclaimed. Acting under the secret orders of Queen Elizabeth I, he was then given command of the *Golden Hinde* and four other ships, carrying 164 men. This fleet left Plymouth, England in November 1577, bound for Spain's great source of wealth, the Peruvian gold mines.

By the time this voyage was over three years later, Drake had logged the world's second circumnavigation and the first one finished by its commander, as Ferdinand Magellan had died before completing his voyage. He had lost four of his five ships and half his men had died. Despite his losses, the journey was considered a grand success, for he and his men had beaten the Spanish in raid after raid, amassing a shipload of Spanish treasure. Known as the "Master Thief of the Unknown World," historian Robert Greenhow wrote:

> *Drake did not hesitate to proceed to the parts of the coast occupied by the Spaniards, whom he found unprepared to resist him, either on land or on sea. He accordingly plundered their towns and ships with little difficulty; and so deep and lasting was the impression produced by his achievements that, for more than a century afterwards, his name was never mentioned in those countries without exciting feelings of horror and detestation. His acts probably contributed to the Spanish Armada's attempt to invade England in 1588.*

By summer 1579, heavily laden with treasure and anxious to return to England as quickly as possible, Drake sailed north along the West Coast searching for the Northwest Passage that would allow him to sail across North America to the Atlantic. Needless to say, he did not find the legendary shortcut he called the Strait of Anian and was eventually forced south by adverse winds off the Oregon coast. He, instead, began to seek the safe harbor he needed to prepare his weathered and battle-scarred *Golden Hinde* for the long trip across the Pacific and home to England. On June 17, he found the harbor he needed.

On June 26, hundreds of Coast Miwoks gathered to ceremoniously welcome Drake and his men. Although it is likely they were making Drake an honorary chief, he chose a markedly English interpretation by reporting that they had crowned him as their leader and abdicated their power. Drake took possession of the land in the name of Queen Elizabeth I and nailed a brass plate on a post with an inscription claiming the land for England. He quickly finished repairs and left by July 23.

As the first Englishman to walk on the North American continent, this brief landing has been cited as the founding of the overseas British Empire, inspiration for their settlement of North America. With the unquestioned importance of Drake's visit to California, the exact location of this stay has become the source of intense analysis and passionate debate among experts and amateurs alike. Much of this debate stems from the mystery surrounding Drake's log. As soon as he handed his log and maps to Queen Elizabeth I on his triumphant return to England, they disappeared. Although most believe that they were not lost but were hidden by the Queen so that they would not fall into enemy hands, they have not surfaced in the intervening four centuries. Hopes for details of his journey withered when Drake died in 1596, without speaking or writing again of his momentous voyage.

Instead, we only have some books published well after Drake's return. One, *The World Encompassed by Sir Francis Drake*, published in 1628, contains observations of his chaplain, **Francis Fletcher**.

Although useful, none of these books contain the invaluable navigational information contained in a log. Despite this lack of data, most experts believe Drake landed at Drakes Bay, Bolinas Lagoon, or San Quentin Cove. This supposition is based, in part, on Fletcher's report that the name "New Albion" (Latin for New England), was chosen because its white banks reminded Drake of England's White Cliffs of Dover. Fletcher described "white bankes and cliffs, which lie toward the sea." Although white cliffs face the sea in all three of these anchorages, experts believe that Fletcher's remark that they "lie toward the sea" more aptly describes the relationship of cliffs to the harbor at Drakes Bay than the other two coves.

Fletcher's journal entries concerning vegetation, wildlife, and local tribes do little to solve the mystery, as all three possible landing sites share similar natural characteristics. His journal does reveal a disappointment with the weather:

> ... notwithstanding it was the height of Summer, and so near the Sun; yet were we continually visited with ... nipping colds ... neither could we at any time in the whole fourteen days together, find the air so clear as to be able to take the height of the Sun or star.

Although his complaints about the cold summer weather and the "thick mists and most stinking fogs" seem to point toward Drakes Bay more than Bolinas or San Quentin, they fall far short of providing conclusive evidence.

Mired in inconclusive evidence, many believed that the discovery by a picnicker in 1936 finally provided the solid evidence everyone wanted. This picnicker found what appeared to be Drake's brass plate near San Quentin Cove, spurring a flurry of excitement and debate. When initial metallurgical tests indicated its authenticity, some thought the centuries-old debate was about to be solved, and that San Quentin would be confirmed as Drake's port. Soon, though, the debate was re-ignited when another man came forward to say that he had found the same brass plate near Drakes Bay three years earlier and had carried it around in his car until finally throwing it out near San Quentin. With the controversy raging, the brass plate was placed in the Bancroft Library at the University of California as one of its prized possessions, while noted historian, Samuel Eliot Morrison, branded the plate a fake and probably a prank. In 1977, an exhaustive analysis concluded that the plate was composed of modern metals that had been rolled and cut in a way that was unknown in Drake's time. In the light of this evidence, most now believe that Drake's brass plate still lies buried in the sand awaiting discovery and inspiring many to keep searching for this illusive proof.

As Drake's quadra-centennial approached, the debate heightened. Drake fans sailed from Plymouth, England across the Atlantic in a replica of the **Golden Hinde** and the *California Historical Society Quarterly* devoted an entire edition to the debate between the three most likely locations: Drakes Bay, Bolinas Lagoon, and San Quentin Cove. To officially mark the quadra-centennial, on June 15, 1979, the Golden Gate National Recreation Area dedicated a non-committal marker near San Quentin stating:

> *Historians have not yet agreed whether Drake's Marin County anchorage was in Drakes Estero, Bolinas Lagoon, or San Francisco Bay.*

More willing to commit to Drakes Bay as the true port, the next day the Sir Francis Drake Quadra-Centennial Committee of the Chamber of Commerce dedicated a bronze plaque near the south edge of Drakes Beach parking lot that reads:

> *On June 17, 1579, Captain Francis Drake sailed his ship* **Golden Hinde** *into the Gulf of the Farallones and the Bay that now bears his name. He sighted these white cliffs and named the land Nova Albion.*

Eventually, analysis turned to the Ming porcelain found in Drakes Bay middens. For years, it had been assumed that it had all been washed ashore in the cargo of the shipwrecked **San Agustin**. In the late 1970s, two separate studies of the 708 fragments from 235 different plates or bowls reached the surprising conclusion that the porcelain had come from two entirely different cargoes. One study focused on its wear and concluded that only some of the fragments had the waterwear identifying a shipwrecked cargo that had tumbled through the surf.

The other study, conducted by Clarence Shangraw, a curator of the East Asian Museum in San Francisco, focused on the evolution of Ming porcelain patterns. In the 16 years between Drake's visit and the wreck of the *San Agustin*, the quality and design of this porcelain changed dramatically. Based on these differences, the Shangraw study again identified two very different groups of Ming porcelain in the Drakes Bay middens. Armed with evidence that Drake left some Ming porcelain with the Coast Miwoks as gifts, many believe that this evidence of two different cargoes of porcelain at Drakes Bay provide the long-awaited proof of the location of Drake's landing.

This evidence was enough for the Marin County Supervisors. In 1994, they passed a resolution declaring Drakes Bay as the site of Drake's landing and formally requesting that the National Park Service to place a plaque there.

However adamantly one would like to believe that Drakes Bay is the site of this historic landing, one must continue to question confusing evidence and seek inconvertible proof. According to prominent Drake scholar Robert Heizer:

> . . . *opinions have not and never will solve the question— only some kind of documentary or archeological evidence to be discovered can solve the problem.*

Until then, the debate continues to enliven many long winter evenings while all await the discovery of the brass plate on a Marin County beach or Drake's log in some forgotten British archive.

Wreck of the *San Agustin*

Rumors of Drake's discovery of a safe harbor on the California coast intrigued the Spanish. Their trade between the Philippines and Mexico was booming, and they were constantly seeking safe harbors along the route. Many believe that Drake's success finding a harbor inspired the Spanish to order **Sebastian Rodriquez Cermeno**, a Portuguese captain trading for Spain, to survey the California coast on his journey to Mexico from the Philippines in 1595. Commanding the *San Agustin*, a Manila galleon laden with a luxury cargo of Chinese silks, spices, and Ming porcelain bound for Acapulco, Cermeno endured both the first of hundreds of documented shipwrecks at Point Reyes, as well as one of the most amazing journeys to safety.

Struggling with a decrepit, heavily-laden ship and a tired, rebellious crew that wanted to go home, Cermeno explored the California coast and eventually anchored the *San Agustin* near the inlet now called Drakes Estero. Within a few days, a November storm beached the ship where it listed and was relentlessly pounded by the furious surf. It soon broke apart, killing several men and dumping precious cargo, some of which was eventually collected by local tribes.

Cermeno salvaged a small, open launch, likened to a large canoe, fortuitously named *San Buenaventura*. Loaded with the 70 surviving crew and the ship's dog, they began the long journey home. After a grueling two-month voyage, remembered as a remarkable feat of seamanship, Cermeno and all crewmembers arrived safely in Acapulco in January 1596. Only the dog had died, eaten by the desperate crew. Despite his amazing voyage to safety, Cermano received no celebratory welcome, for he had not only lost his ship and cargo, but had also failed to find the safe harbor he was ordered to locate.

In 1602, **Sebastian Vizcaino**, one of the survivors of the *San Agustin*, was commissioned to lead a fleet of three ships and 200 men on another exploratory expedition up the coast of California. Leaving in August, and plagued by illness, they voyaged north as quickly as possible, naming everything they saw. On January 6,

1603, the Day of the Three Kings, they sighted a peninsula and named it Punto de los Reyes. Though successfully documenting and naming much of the California coast, Vizcaino sailed by without discovering the nearby San Francisco Bay. According to historian John Robertson:

> For one hundred and fifty years following the Vizcaino failure properly to locate the inner port of San Francisco there was a continuing belief among the Spaniards that somewhere near Point Reyes an inner harbor, great in extent, one suited to the necessities of their Philippine galleons, could be found.

It took another expedition a century and a half later before the Spanish finally found the huge bay they were seeking.

Portola's Inland Expedition

Despite reports of a lovely land populated by friendly tribes, Spain neglected California until the second half of the 18th century. By this time, trade had become an important source of income, and it was evident that the nation controlling California's harbors would reap incredible profits. When England, France, and Russia began to covet California's coastline, the King of Spain knew that it was time to assert his ownership by fortifying the coast. To identify sites for presidios and missions, an overland expedition of 67 men and 100 pack mules left San Diego in 1769. Led by **Gaspar de Portola,** Governor of Baja California, they began walking to the largest known harbor, Monterey Bay. Progress was slow as the expedition had to wait for scouts to identify passable routes before proceeding. Charged with gathering information, engineer Miguel Costanso and Father John Crespi wrote incredibly detailed descriptions of much of California.

Overshooting Monterey Bay, a party of scouts, lead by **Sergeant Jose Francisco Ortega**, and heading for Point Reyes, at last discovered the Bay of San Francisco on November 1, 1769. Although the

18

discovery of the bay was significant, the size of the bay made it impossible for these scouts to follow their orders to explore Point Reyes. Once Ortega's scouts returned, the entire Portola expedition walked along the bay, hoping to continue their journey north. Although they traveled for several days, they never found a place narrow enough to cross and soon turned south again, never reaching Point Reyes. Despite the fact that they never explored the peninsula, the information from the expedition spurred enormous changes.

Missions

Soon after Portola's return, Spain began establishing its presidios and missions. Four presidios were built, first in Monterey and San Diego, with San Francisco and Santa Barbara following. While they were being built, missions were dedicated to convert the tribes and cultivate the land. By 1817, Mission San Rafael was established, and padres began to journey to Point Reyes, intent on enticing the Coast Miwok to the mission. Although Mission San Rafael padres were successful coercing many Coast Miwoks to settle at the mission and begin a life of backbreaking labor, diseases soon began to weaken them. Initially, serious outbreaks of small pox and pneumonia killed many. Those who survived sickened from a wide variety of other diseases, such as colds and measles, while birthrates dropped and infant mortality rates increased at an alarming rate.

Padres at San Rafael, as at missions throughout California, were forced to face the fact that the Coast Miwok were not thriving in their new role as Christian farmers. Since missions were dependent on large numbers of healthy workers for their prosperity, these illnesses foretold their demise.

The deterioration of these missions accelerated when Mexico gained possession of California in 1821. Ownership by Mexico ended the era of Spanish domination that destroyed the self-sufficient, harmonious, centuries-old Coast Miwok way of life. Instead, mission land was granted as enormous, privately-owned ranchos, ushering in the short-lived period remembered as "Old California."

Late Afternoon on Peninsula Hilltop

Wetlands near Bolinas

Ranchos and Boundary Battles

Shortly after Mexico won its independence and possession of California, the powerful mission system was dismantled. Surviving Coast Miwok fled inland or were hired as laborers, and enormous land grants (ranchos) were given to Mexican loyalists. This ushered in "Old California," characterized by fiestas, rodeos, vaqueros (cowboys), food, music, and dancing. In less than three decades, this era was over, replaced by American rule and rapid dissolution of the Mexican ranchos.

As the stage was being set for these sweeping changes, a visitor to Point Reyes would see seemingly endless vistas of land, dotted with the scattered survivors of Mission San Rafael's wild herds of cattle. One might also occasionally glimpse lonely squatters, possibly deserters from whaling ships, who subsisted by planting a few vegetables and fishing, clamming, and hunting. Although the names of these squatters have been largely forgotten, the 1880 *History of Marin County* noted their brief stay at Point Reyes before moving on to other unclaimed land:

> *Whither they have gone no one knows. No trace has been left behind, and they have, probably, all gone to that undiscovered country from whose bourne no traveler hath yet returned, 'unwept, unhonored, and unsung.'*

One exception to this vast sweep of uninhabited land was Point Reyes' oldest settlement, Bolinas. Its remote lagoon had, for many years, made it the perfect secret harbor. Although not documented, it is likely that the 1808 Russian expedition to Bodega Bay that nearly decimated the local otters and fur seals hunted in Bolinas Lagoon. During Spanish and Mexican times, this remote lagoon was used by American, British, and Russian smugglers intent on avoiding tariffs and regulations. Later, when the Gold Rush of 1849 generated a huge market for lumber, Bolinas became the port for nearby timber operations and, briefly, quarrying limestone.

Mexican Ranchos

Soon after Mexico gained possession of California, the breakup of the missions began. Although they were not formally dissolved until 1833, the procedures for allocating their vast expanses of land were codified in the Mexican *Colonization Laws* of 1824 and 1828. These laws allowed Mexican citizens to petition the governor for a specific parcel of land. After an investigation of the petitioner and verification that the requested land was available, the governor could recommend approval by the territorial legislature.

Once the land grant was approved by the legislature, the new grantee was required to conduct an official survey and retain the resulting map. He was also required settle the land after obtaining formal possession of it from a competent local judicial authority who, theoretically, would identify any boundary conflicts with adjacent land grants before conferring possession. In 1833, Mexio passed the *Decree of Secularization*, converting all missions to parish churches and transferring their vast resources, except the churches, to the government. Huge tracts of mission land were now available. Petitions for this free land proliferated and much of it was soon granted to loyal Mexican soldiers and citizens.

Garcia's Rancho

The first Point Reyes land grant was awarded to **Rafael Garcia,** a corporal in the Mexican Army who had completed his required 10 years of service. He petitioned in July 1835 and was awarded two leagues (8911 acres) in March 1836. Named Rancho Tomales y Baulinas, its boundaries were believed to include the Olema Valley from Tomales Bay to Bolinas Lagoon, but were imprecisely described. This lack of accurate details, plus Garcia's failure to survey and locally confirm boundaries before taking possession, set the

22

stage for conflicts that ensued. Although this failure to comply with Mexican requirements was not unusual, its prevalence at Point Reyes contributed to the lengthy court battles that accompanied the dissolution of the ranchos.

Almost immediately after taking possession, Garcia again broke the law by allowing his brother-in-law, Gregorio Briones, to occupy a portion of it, a clear illustration of a casual approach to land ownership. In 1843, Briones attempted to legalize his rights by filing a correction deed stating that he had been living on the land continuously since 1836. By 1846, his appeal was approved, and he was given legal title.

Despite Garcia's failure to follow procedures, he, unlike the other Point Reyes rancheros (ranchers), adhered to the law by actually living on his land. In fact, Garcia had moved there in 1834, two years before it was even granted to him. By 1837, he had built a wood and thatch home near today's site of the National Seashore's Bear Valley Headquarters. Before long, he had built a comfortable home for his family and headquarters for extensive rancho operations, soon consisting of approximately 3000 cattle, 400 horses, and large herds of sheep and hogs. He hired Coast Miwoks to do most of the work. Thriving quickly, the rancho was soon largely self-sufficient. Grains and produce were grown, and a wild steer was slaughtered each day to provide the staple diet of tortillas and beefsteak. Additionally, wool was processed and woven for clothing, and hides were crafted into a wide variety of leather products, including shoes and saddles.

Although virtually self-sufficient, most rancheros throughout California acquired luxuries by trading. Although Mexico had prohibited all trade with foreign ships, the government was incapable of enforcing this law, and much rancho trade was illegally conducted with foreign ships. This smuggling allowed rancheros to acquire luxury items by trading their overabundance of hides, tallow, and produce. Garcia was no exception. His hacienda was adorned with bronze candlesticks, fine candles, artificial flowers, framed engravings, and elegant furniture. It was also supplied with seemingly limitless quantities of wine and champagne. Although it is likely that

Garcia got most of his luxury items through smuggling, he may have obtained some of them from another source—Point Reyes' many shipwrecks.

Whatever the source, Garcia enjoyed the classic "Old California" lifestyle of fiestas, replete with fine clothing, fancy saddles, jewelry, exhibitions of rodeo skills, bull and bear fights, enormous amounts of food, music by fiddling vaqueros, and dancing throughout the night. These celebrations often also included elk hunts, using only rope, a luna (crescent-shaped stone), and knife. Valued for its tallow and hide, elk disappeared from the peninsula within a few decades. Those that survived the frequent hunts swam across Tomales Bay to the safety of the Sonoma County wilderness.

When Mexico lost California to the Americans, Garcia continued to prosper for awhile. Soon after the American takeover, the Gold Rush of 1849 brought floods of prospectors. Where his wild cattle had been valued only for their hides and tallow, he could now sell them to feed hungry gold-seekers, netting as much as $35 each. Unfortunately for him, these prosperous years ended quickly, for, in 1851, the United States passed a law requiring rancheros to prove legal ownership of their land grants. While the Garcias continued to party, their land began to disappear until, after 15 years of litigation, multiple court appearances, and high legal fees, Garcia, had sold all but 3085 acres of his grant at bargain basement prices.

Confused Boundaries

In 1836, another Point Reyes land grant was awarded. This time it was given to an Irishman, **James Berry,** who had become a Mexican citizen and a colonel in their army. His grant, named Rancho Punta de los Reyes, spanned approximately 38,000 acres in the Olema Valley. Although he complied with Mexican law by stocking his rancho with cattle and building a home, he clearly intended to be an absentee ranchero, for he hired Garcia to run his cattle.

A mere two years later, he sold two leagues, nearly 9000 acres, to a sea captain, **Joseph Snook**, an act clearly prohibited by Mexican law and grounds for forfeiture of his entire grant. Aware of the illegality of his sale, Berry wanted to keep the sale secret, but Snook wanted a title and began to investigate his options. He discovered that his only way to obtain title to land he had illegally purchased was to formally "denounce" Berry's ownership on the grounds that he had not occupied it. Snook did this, probably with Berry's approval, and obtained title to 8878 acres of Berry's rancho. He stocked it with 56 head of cattle and, like Berry, hired Garcia to oversee his rancho, paying him $12 per month.

Amazingly, three months after he won title to his land, he, too, illegally traded it! This time, the land went to **Antonio Maria Osio**, administrator of the Customhouse in Monterey and recipient of the Angel Island land grant. Desiring more than Snook's 8878 acres, in 1840, he petitioned for the remaining land on Point Reyes. After three years of delays, he was awarded an additional 48,829 acres. Osio moved his family there while continuing to work in Monterey, serving as justice of the Superior Court from 1840 until 1845, a substitute congressman in 1843, and becoming a San Rafael judge in 1845.

Before long, Osio discovered an amazing tale of unofficial land swaps: When Garcia had transferred his land to his brother-in-law, he began using Berry's land, even building a home there and naming it Rancho Al Punta El Estero! Unconcerned, Berry simply began running his cattle on Snook's property. For awhile, this worked well for all, as there seemed to be plenty of land for everyone. This all changed when Osio bought Snook's land and arrived to find Berry using his land.

Osio sued Berry in 1844 and won. The judge recommended that everyone move back to the land to which they held title. Instead of pushing Garcia out, Berry transferred his property to a friend, **Stephen Smith,** to pay for some debts. Garcia remained on the land that was now Smith's, and Osio was content that his rancho was no longer being encroached.

When the United States took possession of California, Osio left and settled in Baja California. By 1852, he had sold some of his land to **Dr. Andrew Randall**, a prominent San Francisco geologist, politician, and investor. He had come to California in 1849 and was soon appointed Monterey's customs inspector and postmaster. He also won a seat in California's first Legislature and founded the California Academy of Sciences. Soon after he bought Osio's land, Randall hired a foreman and built a home for himself, his wife, and four children, though they seldom occupied it.

Randall also purchased the land Berry had traded to Smith. Smith had sold it to **Bethuel Phelps** for $15,000, and Randall purchased it soon afterward for a whopping (and borrowed) $150,000. At first, his purchases appeared to be promising for, by 1854, his property was assessed at $178,365, including 35,520 acres of land valued at $2 an acre, buildings, wild and tame horses, cattle, and sheep. Unfortunately, he also purchased other large tracts of land throughout California and his debts mounted alarmingly. When a financial depression swept the nation, his creditors, understandably, pressured him for their money. The battle for Point Reyes was about to begin.

Battle for the Ranchos

Confused? The Point Reyes ranchers were too and, in 1844, had asked the Mexican government to investigate titles and clarify ownership. Any progress they may have made untangling claims was lost when the United States gained ownership of California in the 1848 *Treaty of Guadalupe-Hidalgo* that concluded the Mexican-American War. Rancheros lived with uncertainty until 1851, when American laws were passed requiring land grantees to prove legal ownership of their land. Proving this ownership was expensive. When the required surveys and court appearances had been completed, most rancheros had won title to their land but owed a great deal of money. Accustomed to bartering, they had little cash. Unable to pay, many lost their land and new owners moved in to divide and develop it.

Despite his casual transfer of land and migration onto the property of others, Garcia's attempt to prove ownership of his grant was relatively straightforward. Unfortunately, by the time he gained official title from the United States Lands Commission, he had already sold much of it, contingent on receiving his title. As early as 1852, he had begun selling some land and, by 1856, he sold over half of his rancho for less than $2 per acre. By the next year, he had sold an additional 1400 acres, again for less than $2 per acre, leaving little in his possession when his title was officially confirmed.

The land acquired by Randall provided all the elements of a tragidrama, including courtroom conflict, angry creditors, a scheming sheriff, a murder, and a vigilante hanging. By the time the Lands Commission confirmed Randall's ownership in 1855, his ballooning debts were being foreclosed, and he was facing legal action. When one creditor, **Joseph Hetherington,** sued, Randall refused to answer the judge's questions, fled, and was arrested for contempt of court. On July 24, 1856, Hetherington approached Randall in a San Francisco hotel and shot him to death. Hetherington was arrested by authorities, but was almost immediately captured from them by the city's Vigilance Committee. Two days later, he was hanged while a crowd cheered. Randall left his wife, Elizabeth, pregnant with their fifth child and saddled with daunting debts totaling $237,000, in addition to multiple pending lawsuits.

Randall's land was foreclosed and sold, sold, and sold again, each of these three purchasers receiving a deed for the same property from Marin County **Sheriff G. N. Vischer**. In addition to these three purchasers, John Hyatt, Thomas Richards, and Samuel Reynolds, two others, **Dr. Robert McMillan** and Jesse Smith, sued and won the same Point Reyes property through court judgments. McMillan and Smith were also issued deeds by the sheriff, resulting in multiple "legitimate" owners of the same land. It was later discovered that the corrupt sheriff had kept the money he had collected from each of these unwitting purchasers.

Even after it was discovered that the sheriff had duped these claimants, the question of who owned the land remained. Hyatt,

Reynolds, Richards, and Smith joined forces to hire a lawyer. McMillan, the only one wealthy enough to hire the best, hired his own lawyer from the prestigious San Francisco law firm, Shafter, Shafter, Park, and Heydenfeldt. The senior partner of this law firm, **Oscar Shafter,** had gained renown as one of California's foremost title litigation experts. Not surprisingly, the California Supreme Court found in favor of McMillan on May 31, 1858. McMillan never actually enjoyed the land he won. Five months earlier he had transferred the title of two-thirds of his Point Reyes land to the law firm in exchange for $50,000. It is likely that the undisclosed legal costs incurred in the lawsuit were included in this trade.

Although this judgment and trade gave the law firm of Shafter, Shafter, Park, and Heydenfeldt much of Point Reyes, some was still owned by others. Members of the law firm moved quickly to acquire the remaining land by purchasing the portion that was still owned by Randall's widow at an auction for $14,000 and the remaining third McMillan had retained for $20,000. Soon, they owned a majority of Point Reyes for a total expenditure of only $84,000.

Demise of the Garcias

Only Garcia's land remained out of their control and, by 1859, Shafter, Shafter, Park, and Heydenfeldt began legal proceedings to acquire it, claiming their rights to the original Berry Ranch included portions of Garcia's land. The battle dragged on for six years and took all of Garcia's capital. It was not resolved until February 21, 1866, a mere 10 days before Garcia's death. When it was concluded, the boundary between the Shafter and Garcia properties was confirmed as Olema Creek, leaving some of Garcia's land and his hacienda in Shafter hands.

By the time the court battles were over and Garcia was dead, the little that remained of Garcia's rancho was split between his widow, Loretta, and their children. Although Loretta got the largest portion, she did not prosper. By 1872, she almost lost it all when the sheriff threatened to take everything to pay her $396 debt to the local grocery store. On April 17, 1873, tragedy struck when a young blacksmith, Ambrosia Correra, visited Loretta, begging her to marry him. About 60 years old at the time, Loretta was not interested in marrying the young man, and they argued. According to her six-year old adopted daughter who witnessed the incident, Correra shot Loretta and, when she tried to get up, shot her again, this time in the head at close range. She died instantly and, after trying to burn the adobe, he fled to a neighboring home where he emotionally confessed his crime and then shot himself in the head.

This important Point Reyes family was further plagued by bad luck and poor judgment and soon faded from the spotlight. Garcia's children retained little of their inheritance, much of which they sold at bargain prices to the Shafters. His oldest son, Juan, worked as a butcher, bartender, wagon hand for Camp Taylor guests, and lottery ticket hustler. With a weakness for gambling, he was rumored to bet $1000 on a hand and died penniless. Felix, another son, was once a saloon owner and constable, but lost his Olema saloon when he fell behind in mortgage payments. He also died penniless. Garcia's other children either died young or left the area.

The short-lived Mexican rancho era, enlivened by fiestas, rodeos, hunts, music, and dancing, soon ended. Instead, California assumed its role as an important part of the United States. The more structured approach to ownership introduced by the Americans spurred protracted legal battles over the enormous Mexican ranchos. When the battles were resolved, the majority of Point Reyes was firmly in the hands of Shafter, Shafter, Park, and Heydenfeldt, setting the stage for the establishment of a unique dairy empire.

Judge Oscar Shafter with Daughters and Grandchild

A Prolific Pair of Milk Producers

Butter at Its Best

Although Point Reyes ownership battles were complex and dramatic, complete with a murder, a hanging, a pregnant widow, a corrupt sheriff, and courtroom antics, the resulting dissolution of the ranchos and the lawyers who benefited is a story that was repeated throughout California. Almost overnight, enormous expanses of land belonged to America's new privileged class—lawyers. When lawyers, rather than settlers and homesteaders, acquired much of the best land, it radically changed California settlement patterns by severely limiting the availability of inexpensive land.

Settlement patterns at Point Reyes were forever changed when the Shafters acquired it, for their land was not for sale. Instead, by investing large amounts of capital, they quickly developed over 30 tenant-operated dairies, soon the largest dairy operation in California. Settlers, seeking opportunity and inexpensive land, were forced to look elsewhere, for Point Reyes was populated by tenants who had little hope of ever owning their land.

Lords of Point Reyes for 60 years, the Shafter brothers, Oscar and James, and Oscar's son-in-law, **Charles Webb Howard,** established large-scale, high-quality dairies that became prime examples of cleanliness, organization, and success. Amazingly, 13 of these dairies, established between 1857 and 1880, have survived pressures from large competitors and increasingly complex regulations to prosper today as important components of the Point Reyes National Seashore.

Enter the Shafters

Dominating much of Point Reyes history from the Civil War until shortly before World War II, the Shafters were Vermont lawyers who fell in love with the stunning beauty and economic promise of

Point Reyes. Oscar Shafter was the first of the family to come to California, and he had no intentions of staying. Born in 1812 and already a successful attorney, he journeyed to California in 1854 after an unsuccessful bid for governor. California lawyers were getting rich from the booming Gold Rush economy and the dissolution of Mexican ranchos, and he intended to be one of them. With plans to make a great deal of money quickly and return home, he left his wife and three children in Vermont. He had soon established a lucrative law firm and faced a dilemma. Should he remain in California and get richer or return home to his family?

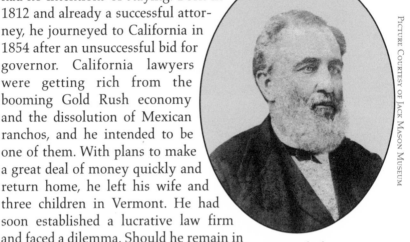

Oscar Shafter

His separation from them became intolerable when his two youngest children, a daughter and the only son he would ever have, died during the winter he was away. Still unwilling to leave the opportunity California offered, by spring, he had convinced his wife, Sarah, to journey to California with his surviving daughter, **Emma**. His family thrived, and he fathered four California-born daughters.

That year, Oscar also convinced his younger brother, **James McMillan Shafter**, to leave Vermont to become a partner in his law firm. Like Oscar, James was already experienced and successful.

James Shafter

Four years younger, he had entered Vermont politics when he graduated from Connecticut's Wesleyan University and had already served in its House of Representatives and as Secretary of State.

They were soon recognized as San Francisco's foremost authorities on title litigation. In addition to profiting from untangling the proliferation of title lawsuits flooding California courts, Oscar and James became members of California's elite political aristocracy. Oscar served as a justice of the California Supreme Court until he retired, his mind crippled by an illness that killed him in 1873. James was elected to the State Senate and served as its president. He also became a University of California regent, a trustee of Stanford University, and a superior court judge. In addition to these offices, both brothers also enjoyed a great deal of the backroom power that charted California's course during its early days of statehood.

When Oscar's oldest daughter, Emma, married Charles Webb Howard, the son of Vermont farmers, in 1861, Oscar erroneously believed that he had found the perfect son-in-law and partner, one who would make Point Reyes' incredible economic promise a reality. Seven years older than Emma, Charles, a liquor distributor in San Francisco, had already organized a trust company, a bank, a railroad, and a vineyard.

Charles Webb Howard

When Oscar and his family moved to a mansion in Oakland, Charles and Emma followed, building a large home next door on land that Oscar had given them. Their first child, Oscar Shafter Howard, was born in 1863 and, by 1865, law firm partners, Park and Heydenfeldt, had agreed to sell their interests in Point Reyes so that Charles could become a full partner. Heydenfeldt sold his one-quarter interest in January for

$35,000 and Park sold his portion for $40,000 in May. As soon as the law partners had sold out, Oscar, James, and Charles were free to use their considerable resources and energies to turn the vast stretches of Point Reyes grasslands into prosperous, tenant-operated dairies.

Shafter Dairy Empire

When the law firm of Shafter, Shafter, Park, and Heydenfeldt acquired Point Reyes, San Francisco grocers and restaurateurs were still importing butter from the East Coast or Chile, and were unhappy with the old, smelly, expensive, and lard-like butter they received. Oscar and James were sure that their land would make them rich and believed that dairying would prosper there.

Delighted with its huge expanses of fog-fed pastureland, they immediately began to plan tenant-operated dairy ranches that would, hopefully, provide the butter San Francisco craved. By February 1857, before the courts had even confirmed their ownership, they bought 20,000 fence pickets. This was the beginning of an enormous fencing project that, by 1875, included 40 miles of fences, requiring the employment of 40 men and the completion of 40 miles of road to transport fencing materials.

In 1857, the Shafters also began the construction of the 2500-acre Home Ranch, an experimental prototype for the rest of their Point Reyes ranches. In late 1859, two fine Durham bulls and four pure-bred Merino rams were brought to stock it. Costing a whopping $1400, they attracted a crowd of admirers at the docks of San Francisco—one of whom offered $1500 for one of the bulls. By early 1860, the first Durham heifer had been imported from Vermont. Costing $500, admiring crowds again gathered on the docks and offered to buy her for more than she cost. During these early years, Oscar and James took an active role in the establishment of their ranches. James accompanied those first fine bulls and rams on their journey to Point Reyes while, early in 1860, Oscar drove 400 ewes (costing $2000) to Point Reyes to breed with the wild sheep of the mission and rancho eras.

Rumored to have purchased the best stock in the state, many watched with interest to see if they would thrive at Point Reyes. Initially not focused solely on dairying, the Shafters experimented raising other stock and cultivating a variety of crops. By spring 1860, the Merino rams and ewes had bred with wild sheep to create a herd of over 2500. This began a brief era of sheep ranching at Point Reyes. By 1866, the Shafters traded their huge herd of sheep for 335 cattle and about $8000. Although citing the drop in wool prices, they also admitted that they hated the constant bleating of more than 9000 sheep and were glad that the magnificent land was finally being used for more dignified cows. In addition to raising sheep, they plowed some land and planted oats, wheat, beets, turnips, and potatoes with some promising successes. The potatoes were large and high-quality; and the beets and turnips were huge, many weighing as much as 40 pounds each. The only failure was the wheat, for the fog impeded its harvesting.

Despite these successes, it was not long before virtually all the land was converted to dairy ranching. Construction of the 31 dairies that would comprise the Shafter empire began in the early 1860s and was nearly completed by 1872. They were named with a letter, beginning with A at the lighthouse and proceeding clockwise around the peninsula with Z Ranch on Mt. Wittenberg. (The only non-alphabetical ranches were south of Bear Valley and were not designed for dairying, but were used for beef cattle and replacement cows.) All dairies were constructed to adhere to a similar layout and included a large home, some with as many as six bedrooms; a milking corral; dairy and horse barns; a calf shed; and pigpens. Some of the larger ones were almost self-contained and had such amenities as blacksmith shops, storehouses, and laundries.

While three of the 10 early diaries produced cheese, within a decade, all Shafter ranchers had stopped cheese production and were producing the more profitable butter. By 1868, the Shafters had 3500 cows on 17 dairies producing 700,000 pounds of butter, almost half of the total in Marin County. While ranches were being constructed, the Home Ranch was used as an experimental station, constantly seeking to breed the finest milk cows and improve the quality of butter manufacture. Scrupulously clean and stocked with every modern convenience, it was designed to be self-sufficient with its own butcher shop, blacksmith shop with a resident blacksmith, and storehouse that rivaled retail groceries. By 1893, Home Ranch was supporting 200 cows and renting for $3500 a year. Today a beef ranch within the National Seashore, it has been occupied and operated by the Murphy Family since 1929.

Financial Risks

The initial outlays to build and stock 31 ranches put an enormous financial strain on even the sizeable Shafter fortune, a sobering reality Oscar learned early, as evidenced by this 1860 letter to his father:

> We have been for the last two years improving our ranch by building houses and fences and have put considerable money into flocks and herds. Everything had to be brought here [San Francisco] and sent over, even to the hay used for horses and working oxen. The drain has been constant on our resources. Last year we paid taxes to the amount of $5000 in gold. This year they will be $3000 more, and they will probably remain at that point for years to come. But the tide already begins to turn. Cattle and sheep not only begin to multiply but to mature.

In 1866, their investments began to pay off when the Shafter dairies took the lead in California butter production. Although some of San Francisco's butter was still imported from the East Coast and Chile, Point Reyes had become San Francisco's favorite source of premier butter. By the 1870s, the Shafter/Howard empire consisted of 31 dairies, each well-stocked with 150 to 170 prime cows, approximately 500 calves a year, and quarterly rent that went straight into their pockets. Estimating that they had invested $500,000, by 1870, their ranches were valued at $2 million. Finally, they could congratulate themselves, for their vision had been realized. Their large and risky expenditures had resulted in well-built, well-stocked dairies that produced the butter demanded by San Francisco's most discerning and affluent residents.

The Contract

By 1861, eight of the ranches had been built and leased. Early tenants were selected from a long list of applicants. As their success was integral to the Shafters' prosperity, these early tenants were selected carefully, both for their drive and financial resources. Prospective tenants needed approximately $2000 ready cash to be approved for a lease. Those selected were, according to Oscar, given a "good and encouraging contract" that set the stage for the tenant system that would dominate Point Reyes for many decades.

This contract provided the land, buildings, farm implements, cows, horses, and pigs for a rent ranging from $1500 to $3000 per year, paid quarterly in advance and in gold. Tenants were charged an additional $20 to $25 a year for each cow. Although in 1870 a good milk cow could be purchased for $40, each cow was expected to produce 200 pounds of butter (selling at 20 to 40 cents a pound), netting tenants $40 to $50 per cow per year.

Tenants were not allowed to raise any animals but the horses, pigs, and cows that were provided. They were also prohibited from selling anything from the land but some of the newborn stock and, of course, the milk and butter they produced. The contract limited the new stock they could sell, for it required the tenant to raise one of every 10 of the calves, hogs, and horses born each year and deliver them to the Shafters.

Although tenants did not get rich, during the good years when butter prices were steady, most were able to make a profit. When butter prices fell and profits decreased, the Shafters also shouldered some of the losses. In 1885, when butter prices fell to 18 cents, tenants were unable to pay the contracted rent and rates were lowered to a level they could afford. By 1891, cow rental had dropped to $17.50 per cow per year. When bad times struck again during the Great Depression of the 1930s, tenants who could not pay were not evicted, but were allowed to continue to operate their dairy until the economy improved.

Despite this compassion and the advantages of renting a well-stocked, well-built Shafter dairy, it was not long before a common complaint echoed throughout Point Reyes: Industrious tenants wanted to own their own land, for they recognized that they would never prosper as renters. Unable to buy their ranches from the Shafters, many eventually left to purchase their own property and, in doing so, established major dairies throughout California. When the ambitious ones left, they were replaced by a constantly changing parade of tenants that would soon challenge the well-being of the Shafter empire.

Dairying Life

The Point Reyes milking season lasted from December until August, with the best milk in the spring and early summer. During these months, milkers were in constant demand. In the off-season, some did other ranch work, while others left to find work in the city. Some milkers were Coast Miwok, while others came from Europe, especially Switzerland and the Azores. Friends or relatives sponsored many of these European milkers. When they arrived, they received only lodging and food until their passage had been paid. Once clear of their debt, they earned the going wage of room, board, and $25 to $30 a month for milking 20 to 25 cows twice a day. Each

Haying Time

ranch also employed a butter maker, often a milker who was able to develop the skill and accurate sense of timing necessary for promotion to the higher-paid position.

After the butter was made, it was stored in a cool cellar until it could be shipped to San Francisco. Although most was shipped to market within a few days, some was saved for the dry seasons of September through November when the demand increased prices. This stored butter was kept fresh by being packed in small wooden casks (firkins) or by covering two-pound rolls in light muslin, packing them in salt brine, and sealing them in barrels. In addition to butter, a large number of hogs were raised at Point Reyes, numbering 2000 in 1870. They were fattened on the whey left over from butter making and shipped by schooner to San Francisco, either live or slaughtered, until 1875, when the railroad changed transportation patterns.

Despite Point Reyes' perfect dairying conditions, tenants and laborers alike led grueling lives of hard work in cold, foggy weather without hope of making much money. Many suffered from "Swiss Diamonds," today widely-known as carpel tunnel syndrome. Although challenging, it was not the working conditions but the drive to own land that pushed many to leave, seeking better opportunities. The Steele family is a perfect example of Point Reyes ranchers who wanted more than the Shafter-Howard empire would offer to them.

The Steele Ranch

One of the Shafters' earliest tenants were the **Steele** brothers, George, Isaac, and Edgar, his wife, Clara, and their cousin Rensselaer, who had come from Ohio in the mid-1850s. Initially settling in Sonoma County, according to legend, Clara Steele milked a wild cow and made cheese, using a recipe she had found in a magazine. The family realized that her cheese was good and began to seek a dairy to operate. When they discovered Point Reyes, with its huge expanses of unoccupied land and lush grasses, they wondered if dairying could thrive there. Could domesticated dairy cows flourish on the land that sustained the scrawny, wild cattle from mission and rancho days?

They decided to take the risk and, on July 4, 1857, leased 10,000 acres for $25 a month from Thomas Richards, one of the many Point Reyes claimants, payable only when the title was settled. Richards also promised to sell it to them for $3 an acre as soon as he owned it. Unfortunately for the Steeles, Richards lost, the Shafters won, and, by July 28, 1858, the Steeles had negotiated a four-year lease from the Shafters. This lease only required a percentage of the calves and hogs born on the ranch in addition to all taxes. When the lease was renewed, rent of $200 a year had been added.

Before long, the Steeles had established three dairies: New Albion, their headquarters; Muddy Hollow; and Laguna Ranches. Despite initially rough conditions, including no fences and inadequate facilities, the abundant grasses nurtured their cows, and they were immediately successful. During their first year, they made an impressive 55,000 pounds of cheese, valued at $15,000. By the second year, they had added $6000 worth of improvements to their dairies, increased their herd to 163 milk cows, and hired nine laborers. Unlike later Shafter-Howard tenants, the Steeles were also responsible for constructing many of their ranch buildings and soon had fine homes for themselves and their employees, in addition to redwood structures with the latest butter and cheese-making equipment.

Remembered as Point Reyes' pioneer dairymen, the Steeles not only proved that dairying could thrive, they also proved that San Francisco was the perfect market for their cheese and butter. They used a schooner that landed at the Limantour Estero to transport their products to San Francisco, selling butter at $1 a pound, and cheese for 27 cents a pound. By 1861, they milked 600 cows and produced an impressive 640 pounds of cheese and 27 pounds of butter a day. Reporting a profit of $10,000, they were soon recognized as the largest cheese-producing dairy in California.

Although wonderfully successful, calling Point Reyes "cow heaven," the Steeles were dissatisfied. They wanted to stay but knew that they must own their land. When they tried to buy it from the Shafters, their offer was refused. Disappointed, they moved on and purchased the 18,000-acre Ano Nuevo Ranch near Pescadero, where they thrived and became one of Shafters strongest competitors. When they left, their three dairies were leased to a series of new tenants, but the decline had begun. By the 1920s, New Albion Ranch had ceased dairying and was growing artichokes, in addition to serving as a central bootlegging station. By the 1940s, Roberts Dairy of San Rafael revitalized it, but by the time the National Park Service acquired it, it had fallen into disrepair and was torn down. By the 1930s, Muddy Hollow Ranch lost its battle against encroaching brush and was turned into a sheep ranch. By the 1960s, it was gone, today marked only by a stand of Monterey cypress. Laguna Ranch was a World War II training camp and is the site of today's National Seashore Hostel.

The Steeles epitomized the early Point Reyes tenants: hard-working, entrepreneurial, successful, but determined to own their land. Like the Steeles, George and Charles Laird left to purchase a dairy that rivaled the Steeles'. **Carlisle Abbott**, went to the Salinas River to develop the third largest dairy in California. Rufus Buell left to buy his own ranch in Santa Barbara County, where he prospered and established the town named after him, Buellton. They became the leading dairymen in California, with ranches competing in size and production to those of the Shafters. Thus, the Shafter-Howard empire played a major role in securing California's place as a leading butter producer by providing an invaluable training ground for the ambitious dairymen who left.

Pierce Ranch

The 2200-acre tract of land at Tomales Point that became Pierce Ranch is unique. The Shafter, Shafter, Park and Heydenfeldt law firm sold it to **Solomon Pierce** in 1858 for $7000 ($3.50 per acre) rather than developing it as another of their tenant-operated dairy ranches. Soon a fine dairy that rivaled the Shafter-Howard ranches, the reason for this exception is unclear. It is possible that, as all were from Vermont, the sale was motivated by friendship.

As soon as Solomon moved his family to his Point Reyes ranch, he began to establish a dairy. The first year, he invested almost $2200 in livestock, including horses, dairy cows, cattle, swine, and two oxen; cleared 400 acres of land; and began dairy operations. During that first year, he produced 4000 pounds of butter and began the ranch's tradition of being one of the best producing dairies at Point Reyes. By 1864, Solomon had moved to Petaluma, leaving his 24-year old son, Abram, in charge of the ranch. Abram only stayed for a year before he leased it and left for an extended trip East. He returned to a dairy that had thrived during his absence. In 1870, it had produced 47,000 pounds of butter, almost twice as much as the second largest producer at Point Reyes.

Abram's return ushered in years of even greater prosperity. By 1878, it had become the largest privately owned and operated dairy in West Marin, milking 300 cows and employing 16. It was also famed for its superior quality of butter. Largely self-sufficient, it had a blacksmith shop, cow and horse barns, a carpenter shop where butter boxes were made, a schoolhouse, a laundry, and a warehouse stocked with a full array of staples. Due to its high production,

The Pierce Ranch

excellent quality, and wide range of amenities, it was often spot-lighted as a prime example of an exceptionally well-managed California dairy.

In 1883, Abram died at the age of 42 of an enlarged heart and other complications. Although his son, William, took over the management of the ranch, he leased it to tenants and spent most of his time in Petaluma, where he managed the local power company. He was the subject of many rumors concerning his romantic involvement with Abram's widow and his stepmother, Mary. William died in his twenties, electrocuted trying to repair a faulty electric line. When he left the Pierce Ranch to Mary, it was valued at $500,000.

After being owned by the Pierce family for three generations, the ranch was sold in 1929 to James McClure. After dairying for a few years, the McClures stopped producing butter and began raising hogs and beef cattle. In 1973, the National Park Service bought the Pierce Ranch and restored it as an educational center designed to illustrate the history of the Point Reyes dairies. Eighteen of its buildings, constructed between 1860 and 1933, are listed on the National Register of Historic Places, many of which are open to visitors. One of Point Reyes' first ranches and recognized as a model of excellence, it now welcomes National Seashore visitors seeking to learn more about the fascinating dairies at Point Reyes.

Olema

As soon as the dairies began to thrive, it became evident that Point Reyes needed a centrally-located town for its supplies, services, and entertainment. In 1857, an initial step toward addressing these needs was made when a hotelier, rancher, and Gold Rush prospector, **Benjamin Winslow**, acquired 574 acres of Garcia's original land grant and built a hotel and saloon and, two years later, a post office. Credited with naming the valley and town, he named his establishment Olema (meaning "coyote" in the Coast Miwok dialect). Today known as the Olema Farm House, it serves fine meals to locals and visitors alike in a lovely, historic setting.

Three years later, Olema had emerged as Point Reyes' commercial center, complete with a post office, grocery store, saloon, butcher shop, livery stable and two hotels. During its early years, the only way to get there was by horseback. By 1867, a wagon road from San Rafael to Olema had been completed, and a stagecoach arrived twice a week. Steady growth continued, and, by 1870, Olema offered three hotels, six bars, and had added a blacksmith shop, wagon shop, dry goods store, and several homes. Despite this progress, it remained a small cluster of buildings surrounded by pastureland, causing the April 24, 1873 *Marin County Journal* to report: "Olema makes no pretensions to being much of a town."

Although not "much of a town," Olema quickly earned a reputation as the place to drink. Another of its saloons was built by **John Nelson**, remembered as one of Olema's most popular founders. Initially operating the mail wagon to San Rafael, he built his hotel, saloon, and restaurant in 1876. Known for his honesty, he soon became the community's unofficial banker: Large amounts of money changed hands safely and discreetly at his saloon. Although he died violently when he was thrown from a runaway buggy in 1898, his hotel remained a family operation for 62 years until it was virtually destroyed by being converted into a barracks during World War II. Languishing until the 1980s, the Olema Inn and Restaurant today welcomes guests with the perfect combination of old-fashioned elegance and modern amenities.

To combat Olema's reputation as the place to drink, Druids Hall was completed in 1885. While this Olema chapter of the United Ancient Order of Druids adhered to principles of mutual support, intellectual growth, and social consciousness, it also served as a temperance society. Druids Hall was the area's meeting place until the 1950s when the Cain Family purchased it. They enjoyed it as a country retreat for many years. Recently restored and furnished with fine antiques, it is today a unique and well-loved bed and breakfast.

Schooners and Steamers

Central to Point Reyes' success as a dairying capital was a solution to its transportation challenges. Water was by far the most efficient mode of travel, and by 1868, a number of steam and sail schooners were anchoring in its protected esteros and bays. They left for San Francisco heavily laden with butter, hogs, calves, lambs, and agricultural products, and returned loaded with food, supplies, equipment, feed, grain, and redwood. Before long, over a half dozen small private wharves had been built, the largest of which was a 200-foot long pier with rails and a slaughtering shed in Drakes Estero. Although the schooners provided an excellent transportation solution, ranchers still faced a long journey over rough trails, often so muddy in the winter that four horses were required to pull a light wagon. Adding to overland difficulties were the many gates that had to be opened and closed during each journey.

Steamers soon replaced most of the feisty little schooners throughout California, and, in 1870, a new, large steamer, *Monterey,* began weekly trips between San Francisco and Tomales Bay, with a stop at Drakes Bay. It left San Francisco at 4:00 every Tuesday and returned every Wednesday evening, landing on the south bank of the creek where the road to Inverness leaves Highway One. Freight charges on this new steamer were 50 cents for each 100 pounds of butter and each hog or calf.

One exception to this trend toward steamers was the *Point Reyes*, purchased by Charles Webb Howard's tenants in the early 1900s. The last of the Point Reyes butter schooners, it made frequent Point Reyes-San Francisco trips until the early 1920s. Its later years saw a tragedy, as reported by the December 1, 1932 *Marin Journal:*

> *David Colvin, owner and master of the freight schooner, **Point Reyes,** was found dead on his boat this morning. Colvin had shot himself through the head.*

Despite the convenience of this sea transport and the expert local knowledge of their skippers, these ships were not immune to the

Butter Schooner *Point Reyes*

hazards of the point's dangerous coastline. In 1878, the **Fourth of July** wrecked, and all aboard died. Twelve years later, the **Nettie Low** capsized and was pounded to pieces by the furious surf in an hour. Amazingly, all hands survived. According to the report of Engineer John Low:

> *A sudden puff of wind with a twist to it like a cyclone struck the boat and careened her. She was soon on her beam ends. All of us were on deck except the Portuguese who was in the cabin. So slowly did the boat go over he had time to climb out and we all five scrambled upon the rail. Then the lifeboat floated and we all got in and rowed to shore.*

Although Point Reyes ranchers enjoyed decades of successful, though challenging, sea transport, they watched enthusiastically as efforts to build a railroad gathered momentum. They hoped that the nation's most convenient transportation link would soon serve their sparsely-populated peninsula.

46

The Partition

Soon after law firm partners Park and Heydenfeldt relinquished their shares to the Shafters and Howard, Oscar, James, and Charles began to discuss dividing their property. By the middle of 1869, the Point Reyes ranches had been partitioned, giving each partner approximately 18,000 acres. Although the parcels were intended to be equal, it is generally accepted that Charles got the best pasture-land and that James' portion was worth more. In an 1875 assessment, the following values were assigned to each section: Oscar's parcel was valued at $244,938; Charles' parcel: $258,718; and James' parcel: $337,794 (including the remainder of Berry's rancho near Bolinas, valued at $65,000). Even though legally divided, the Shafter-Howard ranches were still considered to be the largest single operation in California, owning one-sixth of the 25,000 dairy cows in its major dairying regions.

Oscar's dream was to retire and move to San Rafael to supervise his ranches. He had never particularly liked practicing law and had seen it as a way to acquire the things he and his family wanted. In a letter that he wrote to his father in 1860, he said,

> I have worked like a dog. . . . I never liked it and kept myself to it for twenty years by vigorous and unsparing self-lashings.

Despite these feelings, he continued to practice. When it appeared that he might be able to finally retire, he, instead, agreed to run for the California Supreme Court. When he won, he gave up the idea of operating his own ranches and convinced Charles to give up his liquor business to oversee them. Unfortunately, Oscar was not able to serve on the Supreme Court for long. He was forced to resign in 1869, suffering from insanity that is now suspected to be the result of inadequate circulation to his brain. He attempted to restore his health by traveling but died in Italy in January 1873.

Under terms of the 1869 partition, James got ownership of the Home Ranch and surrounding dairies. Although he and his family visited the ranches often and spent many summer vacations there, they lived a life of affluence and prestige in San Francisco, where he invested heavily in a variety of risky business schemes. In 1875, he gave one of his two sons, Payne, a large home and 2235 acres near Olema as a birthday present. Payne's passion was horse racing, and he soon had a racetrack and stable that employed as many as 30 grooms, jockeys, and trainers. Comfortable in his role of local squire, Payne's home became a popular gathering place for San Francisco's affluent sporting crowd.

The partition gave Charles the best pastureland. He also got the 7739-acre Bear Valley Ranch, near the site of Garcia's adobe and today's National Seashore headquarters and visitors' center. Like Home Ranch, Bear Valley, initially called the W Ranch, became both ranch headquarters and a showplace. For awhile, Charles was an actively-involved manager of construction and dairy operations. During these years, he spent a great deal of time at Point Reyes, while Emma languished in their Oakland mansion with their rapidly-increasing brood of children. Despite his involvement with the ranches, he still had time to invest with James in some risky business ventures and had soon amassed some large debts.

When Oscar died, Charles was not only financially vulnerable, but also responsible for Oscar's widow, Sarah, and their four adolescent girls. To compound his problems, he had an unhappy wife who saw him as indifferent to her and disloyal to her beloved father. When, in spring 1874, he proposed a trip to Europe for the entire family, Emma was thrilled. Unfortunately, as soon as the family was settled in Dresden, Germany, Charles announced that he was needed in California and left. He did not see his family until 18 months later when a disgusted Emma gave up waiting for him in Europe and brought the children home.

It was not long after Emma arrived home that she discovered why Charles had left: Ignoring his promise to Oscar to manage the ranches, he had long been positioning himself for the presidency of the Spring Valley Water Company. He was successful and was soon devoting his energies to the water company and other San Francisco interests, including the muckraking magazine, *The Wasp*. From then on, Charles' involvement with Point Reyes decreased and more and more responsibility was placed in the hands of his able superintendent, William Abbott.

Railroad Era

Railroads were connecting towns all across America, virtually replacing other modes of transportation. In California, rails soon replaced a vibrant water-borne shipping industry. Many believed that Point Reyes' thriving dairies deserved a railroad. James Shafter took the lead voicing this need, and, on December 19, 1871, he and a group of businessmen incorporated North Pacific Coast Railroad with the intent of getting narrow gauge railroad service to Point Reyes. Although this railroad would clearly serve the ranchers, it also addressed the Shafter-Howard agenda, for it extended to the rich Sonoma County redwood forests where they owned timber rights.

When this railroad was incorporated, directors were named, with James Shafter as president. James only served as president for a few weeks and was soon replaced by an ambitious and passionate director, Austin Moore, who lobbied ranchers and businessmen to encourage the Marin Board of Supervisors to support a bond to finance the line. He was successful, and, on January 29, 1872, just over a month after the railroad's incorporation, the Board voted to issue a $160,000 bond to build it.

The project was threatened when the Chief Engineer, George Black, resigned, convinced that building a railroad to the redwood forests was expensive, extremely difficult (if not impossible), and stupid. Despite his widely-shared doubts and rapidly-escalating costs, already estimated at $333,000, Moore persevered. He was successful convincing the Sausalito Land and Ferry Company to donate 30 acres along the shore of Richardson Bay as well as gaining the support of the wealthy United States Senator Milton Latham. With this donation and Latham's backing, he stemmed doubts that had almost squelched the project, and, by 1873, a celebration, complete with a banquet and speeches, marked the beginning of construction.

Three construction teams, comprised of approximately 1300 Chinese men and 200 supervisors, began working toward one another. A difficult project, it was slightly simplified when the decision was made to shorten the route to terminate the line at the timber-rich Russian River rather than continuing all the way to the Gualala River. Less than two years later, on January 7, 1875, the line was completed from Sausalito to Tomales, while it took until over two more years for it to reach its Russian River terminus.

Point Reyes Station

James Shafter acquired Olema lots, many of them from sheriff's auctions, in preparation for the land boom he expected once the railroad arrived. Everything changed when, in 1875, the North Pacific Coast Railroad bypassed Olema. It stopped, instead, two miles to the north, where entrepreneur and dentist, **Dr. Galen Burdell,** owned 960 acres of vacant land, a present from his wife. Burdell began building and, in less than a decade, Point Reyes Station, had replaced Olema as the commercial center of the region.

When the first train arrived on January 7, 1875, Point Reyes Station was a cow pasture. Early arrivals were appalled to find nothing—no hotel, no restaurant, no saloon, not even a small shop to buy a snack. Although only two miles away, Olema was impossibly far away for these tired and hungry passengers for there was no transportation linking the station to the town. Burdell wasted no time building a hotel and saloon across from the station. By 1880, Point Reyes Station also had a blacksmith shop, livery stable, butcher shop, and school. A post office was completed by 1882, and its first store opened in 1883. Despite these improvements, it was still clearly a railroad town with a turntable, water tank, cattle pens, and, later, quarters for workers that dominated the center of town.

For awhile, Burdell was able to maintain his monopoly by leasing, rather than selling, town lots. Determined to keep the whiskey flowing at his saloon, lease contracts prohibited the sale of alcohol at any but his establishment. Those who wanted to drink anywhere else went to one of Olema's many saloons. His monopoly did not last. By 1908, when his son, James, filed the town's first tract map, it was owned primarily by ambitious and hard-working Swiss. They had arrived as dairymen, but had given up their leased ranches to make their fortunes as merchants and bankers. By 1915, Louis Grandi and his sons, Ren and Ennio, incorporated, bought the hotel block, and opened Point Reyes' largest business where one could buy anything from fine furnishings and elegant clothing, to shovels and cattle feed. Not simply a store, it was also a hotel and a dance-hall that was used on Sundays as a church.

Railroad Woes

While the completion of the line to Tomales was celebrated "with the ringing of cow bells and the firing of guns," worry permeated the offices of the North Pacific Coast Railroad, for costs had far exceeded the $160,000 in County funding and threatened the fortunes of its investors. In the face of these financial worries, Senator Milton Latham took over as president. Thankful of his vast fortune, investors relaxed and spending accelerated. The railroad soon owned

Main Street, Point Reyes Station

bright yellow passenger cars, gleaming locomotives, modern stations, an ornate private car to entertain investors, and two elegant steamers to transport passengers from Sausalito to San Francisco.

In 1877, financial concerns resurfaced when railroad income failed to offset its enormous expenditures, and the fortunes of investors were threatened once again. The decline continued and Latham's fortune dwindled until, by 1880, he and the railroad were broke. Latham lost everything and the railroad was sold. Latham was not the only one to lose. A number of locals had invested their fortunes in the railroad, most notably James Shafter. Faced with the failure of his railroad investment, he desperately sought a moneymaking scheme that would repay his rapidly-growing debts.

Signs of Change

Initially, the Shafter-Howard dairies were rich with spacious, well-equipped buildings and the finest stock. They quickly emerged as the leaders in the California dairy industry, a role they retained into the 1890s. But, by the end of the 19th century, restlessness with the Shafter-Howard domination of Point Reyes was brewing, and the clouds of change were gathering on the horizon. As early as 1880, the *History of Marin County* reported:

> *The land is owned by one or two men, and hence there are no homes made. Renters stop awhile and then go, making no improvements. Were all this land put upon the market, and sold to actual settlers ... the owners would make their homes look homelike instead of allowing them to remain bleak, barren, and uninviting. . . . . Its industry is stable and will always cause it to be prosperous. Only one thing is lacking, and that is that farmers should be land owners instead of renters. Then would be inaugurated an era of prosperity little dreamed of now. This time will come sooner or later.*

That time was quickly approaching, as the Shafter-Howard empire began to crumble.

The Crumbling Shafter-Howard Empire

Despite their boundless optimism about the promise of Point Reyes, James, Oscar, and Charles did not get rich from it. Although they all lived the opulent lifestyles of the wealthy of San Francisco, financial concerns about their ranches plagued them. To further complicate these worries, both James and Charles invested in unwise money-making schemes that placed them in imminent danger of bankruptcy.

Worried about their growing debts, they began to explore other sources of income from their land. They explored for oil, prospected for gold, and tried to sell their timber. They also sought to develop sportsmen's clubs and exclusive residential communities. One of these developments, the Point Reyes Shafter Colony, planned to stretch along 20 miles of oceanfront, was advertised in 1879 as "Eden on Earth." They failed in every attempt to use their land to replenish their fortunes. Point Reyes remained a sparsely-settled dairying community, and the Shafter-Howard coffers continued to suffer from too many ranch expenses, too many unlucky investments, and too many ideas that simply did not work.

James Shafter's Estate

In the 1870s, led by the Big Four, Leland Stanford, Collis P. Huntington, Charles Crocker, and Mark Hopkins, entrepreneurs throughout the country were making their fortunes building railroads. James Shafter believed that the North Pacific Coast Railroad would make him rich, and he invested heavily. He was wrong. Instead, it threatened to bankrupt him. Unable to pay his creditors, he tried to shore up his ailing financial empire, including a $75,000 personal debt to Leland Stanford, by developing a town. James named his 640 acres on Tomales Bay Inverness in honor of his Scottish ancestors. Lots were offered for sale, plans to build an

$80,000 hotel were announced, and expensive sales brochures were distributed. James died in 1892 before these plans to regain his fortune could come to fruition.

The news that he had left enormous unpaid debts from numerous bad investments shocked many. Most shocked were his three children who had led a life of plenty and were now left with less than nothing. With finances in total disarray and unpaid debts looming, the court assigned James' 33-year old daughter, **Julia Shafter Hamilton,** to manage the heavily mortgaged land she and her two brothers had inherited. Julia spent the rest of her life struggling to pay off their father's large debts, seldom more than a step ahead of impatient creditors.

Julia Shafter Hamilton

Julia, the youngest of James' children, was clearly the most capable of handling the challenges they had inherited. By the time her father died, Julia had been married to **Alexander Frederick Fisher Hamilton ("Jack")** for three years. While she struggled to free the estate from its daunting debts, her marriage failed. Jack, who loved the fine and expensive things in life and drank too much, spent Julia's desperately-needed money. Her anger over his waste of her money was so intense that it was not uncommon for her to lash out at him with her tongue, or even her briefcase. He responded by mocking her. In 1895, Julia left him, taking all community property, but, by 1906, they were living in the same home, still arguing.

Vowing to escape from debt, Julia decided to continue the development of Inverness that her father had begun. Unfortunately, she faced some unexpected challenges. First, she had to pay off the $75,000 mortgage on the land held by Leland Stanford before she could even begin to sell it. By 1905, she had repaid the debt, and the land was hers to sell. She subdivided the 640 acres into 10,000 lots, with a projected profit of $1.5 million. An ambitious marketing effort was launched, complete with slogans and expensive brochures. Unfortunately, just as her marketing plan was being launched, the April 18, 1906 earthquake dashed her hopes of escaping from her father's debts.

Earthquake

Everyone at Point Reyes was shaken early on the morning of April 18, 1906. The peninsula leapt 15 feet in 40 seconds when the stresses along the two continental plates caused a mighty earthquake. The San Andreas Fault cracked along Tomales Bay, Olema Valley, and Bolinas Lagoon, damaging towns and ranches alike. The southeast corner of the barn of Bear Valley Ranch, now used as National Seashore archives and meeting rooms, was sheared off at an angle; the path to the ranch house moved 15 feet; a row of raspberry bushes leapt 14.5 feet; and a fence shifted 15.5 feet. Despite damage to ranches, devastation was most obvious in towns, where a train

Inverness Beach Houses after 1906 Earthquake

preparing to leave Point Reyes Station tipped over, and, in Inverness, homes fell off their foundations, water mains broke, and the post office collapsed. Also, James's son, Payne, reported that a creek reversed direction and a cow was swallowed up in the crack of the earth, only her tail waving above ground, but his reputation as a storyteller led many to question this tale.

Although the total losses were far less than were suffered by densely-populated San Francisco, the incident left a lasting residue of concern among many locals. They could no longer ignore the threat of future earthquakes, for this shift had unmistakably defined the crack in the earth's surface. It left a clear warning that the peninsula was mobile and that subsequent earthquakes would surely shake them up again as it inched its way north.

No Relief for Julia

The 1906 earthquake badly damaged newly-built homes at Inverness. It also clearly demonstrated that Inverness was perched

1906 Earthquake Tipped This Train at Point Reyes Station

Inverness Store after 1906 Earthquake

precariously on a major fault, killing Julia's dreams of a town of 10,000 and the restoration of her fortune. Although the large community of fine homes Julia envisioned never materialized and her indebtedness grew, she did continue to improve Inverness by piping in water and clerking in its first school. Unfortunately, her efforts to provide needed improvements were inadequate, and it was not long before Inverness residents were disappointed and resentful. Despite her failure to develop Inverness as promised, it eventually became the perfect home for retirees and a great summer escape for city-weary workers. Known for its strong family values, it was an early stronghold of the Temperance Movement and became known for its community events, including beach bonfires, community sings, and Fourth of July picnics.

In addition to her attempts to develop Inverness, Julia considered other schemes, such as a condensed milk factory, timbering, the revival of the charcoal industry, a large-scale fishing enterprise, a limestone mine, and an electric car transportation system. When none of these schemes proved to be lucrative, she was forced to sell portions of Olema Valley farmland to avoid bankruptcy. Although these sales allowed her to pay the interest on her loans, she was never able to clear the estate of its debts.

The ranches suffered during these debt-ridden years. She tried to sell some of them, but found no buyers. Unable to sell them, she struggled, unsuccessfully, to maintain them. As the dairies fell into disrepair, the morale of the tenants suffered. The ambitious ones left, marking the end of era when Shafter dairies led California in innovation and production. In a letter to her husband, now part of the Jack Mason Museum collection, she lamented:

> So many repairs are needed and lumber is so high that my heart sinks within me. It is nothing but pay out money all the time and nothing to show for it – until I am sick at heart and frightened and worried.

As conditions worsened, and pleas for veterinary services and fence repair went unanswered, tenants began to rebel by cheating on her. They took her bulls to market, bought them back, and gave her the bill. They also defied her by shooting deer, an activity prohibited in their leases. By the 1920s, Julia had totally lost control of her ranches. When tenants' morale was lowest, Prohibition propelled Point Reyes into eminence as the perfect entry point for illegal alcohol. Isolated, sparsely settled, and rich with bays and private wharfs, liquor was easily smuggled from Canadian ships waiting three miles offshore to small boats that landed in quiet coves. Liquor was then loaded onto trucks that swiftly traveled dark, deserted roads toward speakeasies in San Francisco and Sacramento. According to local historian **Jack Mason**:

> Mrs. Hamilton's ranches were a smuggler's paradise, vast and lone. Across Point Reyes the rum flowed like honey, only faster. It came in small boats on Limantour Spit at night, was hauled up the hill in wagons, and stashed under the straw in Mrs. Hamilton's great old barns.

Rumrunners were not smugglers sneaking to Point Reyes, but were the tenant dairymen who had discovered that they could make far more at smuggling than dairying. It was not long before they stopped pleading to Julia for fences, young bulls, and medicine for their cows—for smuggling had replaced dairying as their major source of income.

In 1924, Julia borrowed $160,000, using her ranches as security. In October 1929, when everyone seemed to be making fortunes, she borrowed an additional $144,000. Unfortunately three weeks after this second loan, the stock market crashed, ushering in the Great Depression. When she was late for her first payment, officers at her bank panicked and gave her 15 days to sell her ranches. By this time, Julia was 70 years old, bedridden most of the time, and no longer able to fight. Within a week, she had sold all her ranches to real estate agent **Leland Stanford Murphy** for $255,000 plus assumption of her bank debt. She died seven years later on June 24, 1936. Although she failed to recover her family's fortunes, she struggled all her adult life to do so, and, according to National Park Service Historian **Dewey Livingston**, spent her life settling debts in a "fair and proud manner."

Charles Howard's Estate

Charles promised his father-in-law, Oscar, that he would quit his San Francisco job and devote his attention to their ranches. He did as promised for awhile, but, by 1875, his interest had strayed and he hired a superintendent to oversee them. Instead, he focused on a variety of interests, including the presidency of Spring Valley Water Company, his timbering investments on the Russian River, a silver mine in Nevada, and railroad stock.

As his unlucky investments drained away his resources, he was forced to borrow on his ranches to keep creditors at bay. He did not share his financial troubles with his family. It was only when foreclosure loomed, and the sheriff threatened to sell the ranches at auction, that Emma learned of the seriousness of their financial troubles. She was furious and, although the foreclosure was averted, she left Charles. At this time, she also pushed her four children away from her and sent all but young Harold, whom she left in the care of a nurse, to boarding schools in the East.

When they became adults, Oscar and Maud continued to let Emma support them. Frederick Paxton moved to Bear Valley Ranch to become a gentleman farmer, and the youngest, Harold, exhibited the dark temper that would keep him in mental institutions for most of his life. Though distanced from her husband and children, Emma maintained an active social life, supporting good causes and hosting celebrated Sunday afternoon receptions until 1904, when, weary of the social whirl, she moved to a small home in Inverness.

Emma blamed Charles for all of her woes, even her father's death, contending that disappointment with him had sparked Oscar's insanity. Charles nursed a strong resentment of Emma and spent the last years of his life getting revenge. He convinced Emma's mother, Sarah, to change her will in his favor, sold timber on her land, and, most insulting, formed an investment company with their children to which he left all family assets when he died in 1908. When Emma learned that she had inherited nothing and that it had all gone to her children, she was enraged and immediately sued her children for her half of the estate. Although she won this suit, she lost any remaining connection with them.

The inheritance she won was hardly worth the battle, for it consisted of heavily mortgaged land. Upon her death in 1916, her four children fought over the estate. While Fred Paxton remained at Bear Valley Ranch, the other adult children stayed away. Young Oscar was in New York City trying to succeed as a songwriter; Maud was in Europe, living on a family allowance; and Harold was in and out of mental hospitals and trouble with the police.

Despite her disinterest in the ranches, Maud resented Fred Paxton's unwillingness to reveal his ranch income and fought to divide all the land equally. After months of arguments and court hearings, she won and, by 1919, the ranches were divided between Charles' and

Emma's four children. Almost immediately, they each sold their portion to **John Rapp**, a wealthy San Franciscan who had just sold his family's successful brewing business. As soon as Rapp acquired the ranches, he placed them on the market. They soon sold, netting him a sizeable profit. The sale of these ranches hastened the inevitable break-up of the Shafter-Howard empire. Finally, some were owned by the ranchers themselves.

Oscar Shafter's Estate

Although Oscar was the first of the partners to die, his lands remained in the family the longest. When his ranches were sold in 1939, the Shafter-Howard empire ceased to exist. After Oscar's death in 1873, Charles administered them until his death in 1908. They were then managed by a holding company until 1939 when they were sold—two ranches to tenants and the rest to **Leonard David,** a San Francisco real estate developer.

With the sale of Oscar's ranches came the end of an era. From 1857 until 1939, the Shafter-Howard partnership had dominated dairying in Point Reyes. Initially well-built, efficiently organized, and stocked with the finest cows and bulls, their consistent high quality catapulted Point Reyes into the spotlight for its premier butter. Unfortunately, as soon as the Shafter-Howard fortunes declined, the dairies languished. Slowly, buildings sank into disrepair, stock sickened, ambitious tenants left, and operations stagnated, casting a dark shadow over the Point Reyes dairies. It was only when they were sold that new energy was infused into them. Despite sympathy for the sorrows of the Shafters and Howard, most agreed that the time for new owners was long overdue and welcomed this change with optimism.

Change: Too Little; Too Much

In addition to the increasing disrepair of the ranches, Point Reyes' fine natural pasture was changing. Overgrazing, plus the introduction of non-native grasses, hurt the grasslands. Slowly, brush, thistle, and broom took over. In response, many ranchers began to experiment with supplemental feed, such as hay, corn, barley, wheat, oats, sugar beets, carrots, potatoes, and squash, to extend the milking season. When research at the turn of the 19th century proved that cows fed alfalfa produced twice as much buttermilk as those fed entirely on grasslands, many began buying feed from the Central Valley, abandoning their fields. Unfortunately, as prices rose, many were forced to look again to their pasturelands and try to reclaim them from decades of damage.

Although California lagged far behind other parts of the nation enforcing agricultural sanitation requirements, by 1915, California passed the Pure Milk Law that mandated pasteurization. This requirement ended butter production at Point Reyes dairies. Instead, tenant ranchers trucked their milk to the Point Reyes Cooperative Creamery, where it was made into butter, cheese, condensed milk, and dry milk powder. Soon, additional regulations impacted the dairies as the Division of Animal Industry implemented disease control procedures, tuberculosis testing, and meat inspection and other regulatory agencies monitored sanitary standards and began grading milk. These regulations challenged Point Reyes dairymen, especially when the ranches were still owned by the financially-troubled Shafter-Howard partnership. Eventually, under new ownership, many were able to achieve Grade A status for their revitalized dairies and, today, continue to hold this prestigious designation.

The dissolution of the Shafter-Howard empire illustrates the sorrows of a family whose passion and vision for an incredible land was overshadowed by unwise investments, unhappy marriages, and unfortunate circumstances. Most would agree that Point Reyes dairies benefited from the large sums they invested during their meticulous development. They would also agree that new owners with money to invest were needed to overcome the prevailing stagnation.

Lighthouse and Shipwrecks

From the earliest history, the wary mariner, skirting the coast of California to the west of Drakes Bay, has known and shunned a certain bold headland, shrouded for the most part in fog, but in clear weather revealed to him in all the awfulness of its rocks and precipices and perpetually churning waters, Punta de los Reyes—point of the kings. The Spanish navigators . . . did well to fear it. God help the hapless mariner who drifts upon it!

San Francisco Chronicle, September 25, 1887

The rugged magnificence of Point Reyes' coastline has awed seamen. It has also terrorized many. From California's earliest recorded maritime history, tales of blinding fog, howling winds, sheer precipices, and heavy surf have filled ships' logbooks. Further complicating the challenges of this dangerous coast, the water directly offshore is often so deep that the bottom cannot be sounded to identify location.

For hundreds of ships, this rough peninsula has been the site of disaster. Beginning with its first documented wreck in 1595, few ships were immune. As soon as trading began to flourish along the California coast, shipwrecks were recorded with regularity. Some, like Cermeno, believed that they had discovered a safe harbor and anchored at Drakes Bay, only to be jettisoned onto the beach by storm-driven waves. Others passed too close to the offshore reefs and were driven onto them, pinioned, and battered by the angry sea. Yet others headed straight into the rocks, believing, until the shocking impact, that they were entering the Golden Gate.

As the California coast became more populated, the incidence of shipwrecks increased. Beginning with the wreck of **Ayacucho** in 1841, there were major shipwrecks almost every year for a century.

Captained by Jose Yves Limantour, a naturalized Mexican citizen born in France, the *Ayacucho* was sailing from Mexico to San Francisco heavily-laden with luxury goods. Limantour overshot the Golden Gate and ran aground on the spit that still bears his name. Leaving his cargo on the beach, he got directions from friendly Coast Miwoks and journeyed to San Francisco. As soon as he arrived, he hired a crew to recover his cargo, but gave them such inaccurate directions that they searched Bolinas Lagoon instead. Next, Limantour led an overland expedition to recover his cargo himself, but got lost and returned, still empty-handed. Finally, John Reed, Marin County's first Mexican land grantee, led Limantour to his cargo. A footnote to the story of the namesake of the well-known Point Reyes spit: In the 1850s, Limantour fled to Mexico with illegally gained wealth. He used forged documents to claim over 600,000 acres, including half of San Francisco, and sold them for between $250,000 and $500,000.

While Limantour's wreck is remembered for his series of navigation failures, General Sherman's 1853 journey to Point Reyes is remembered for his dauntingly bad luck. Initially shipwrecked on Duxbury Reef, he boarded a lumber schooner at Bolinas to finish his trip. This ship was wrecked also, giving Sherman the record for having been shipwrecked at Point Reyes twice in 24 hours!

Throughout the centuries, clippers, schooners, modern tankers, and airplanes faced disaster in the furious surf along the foggy coast. It brought death to over 100 crewmembers and passengers and the loss of millions of dollars worth of rich cargoes of spices, perfumes, porcelains, silks, lumber, gold, dynamite, and, more recently, oil.

Land Negotiations Postpone Lighthouse

With the rapidly-increasing commerce along California's coast and the growing number of shipwrecks, the United States government moved quickly to prevent additional losses by building lighthouses. In 1849, a survey to recommend lighthouse locations ranked Point Reyes second in importance of the 16 sites identified. Despite its high ranking and reputation as the West Coast's windiest and foggiest location, a light at Point Reyes was not included in the first eight that were funded.

By 1852, a Lighthouse Board was established. This change spurred needed lighthouse improvements, and, by 1854, Congress had appropriated $25,000 for the lighthouse at Point Reyes. Funding included $10,000 for the light and $15,000 for construction. Initially, things moved quickly. Captain Campbell Graham was authorized to proceed with construction as soon as possible, and a map published in September 1854 included the lighthouse. By June 1855, Graham had arranged a contract to build the keeper's home and signal tower for $10,500. Unfortunately, the title to the land had not yet been obtained, and, by October, all work was suspended.

Efforts to gain title to the land were initially complicated by courtroom battles over ownership of Point Reyes. During the winter of 1855-56, one claimant, Thomas Richards, agreed to sell 83 acres for $1500. Unfortunately, when the dust settled, Richards did not own the land and negotiations had to begin again, this time with the law firm Shafter, Shafter, Park, and Heydenfeldt. Negotiations stalled when the Shafters demanded what was considered to be an exorbitant price for the land. Conscious of the political power they held, government officials were unwilling to condemn and seize it. Instead, frustrated California U.S. Senator William Gwin requested additional funding, describing the problem to the Senate on April 19, 1860:

> There is a lighthouse that ought to have been built at Point Reyes years ago. We had an appropriation of $25,000. The parties owning the ground, knowing the necessity of having a lighthouse there, asked $25,000 for three and two-thirds acres, the amount of the entire appropriation, when it was not, in fact, worth twenty-five cents an acre.

Although Congress agreed to appropriate an additional $40,000 for the lighthouse and $2500 for a fog signal, negotiations continued without resolution. When government officials offered $5000 for land they considered worthless for anything but a lighthouse, the law firm responded by offering to sell 23 acres for $10,000. Urgency was re-ignited in 1868 when the San Francisco Board of Marine

Underwriters identified losses totaling $750,000 since 1860 that could have been prevented if a light had been shining at Point Reyes. Also that year, the Shafter-Howard partnership warned the government that they were considering selling the disputed land to another party. Finally, the government was spurred to action, and, by November 1868, condemnation proceedings began. Before they were completed, the Shafter-Howard partnership made a counter offer of $6000 that was accepted. On July 28, 1869, a deed was signed that gave the government 83 acres at the point, a convenient embarcadero on Drake's Bay, and access to firewood, fuel, water, and granite. And, at last, 15 years after Congressional approval, the building began.

Building the Lighthouse

By 1869, over $49,000 had been budgeted for the Point Reyes Lighthouse, and Congress would be forced to allocate another $45,000 before it was complete. Although the delays were frustrating and costly, there was one positive outcome, for much had been learned about the California coast in the intervening years. Initially planned for the top of the bluff, a mid-cliff location, 225 feet above sea level, was selected—for it had been determined that fogs frequently obscured the top of the bluff.

Although the mid-cliff location selected was clearly superior, it made construction far more dangerous, difficult, and costly. A tramway with carts operated by cables was built to carry tools and materials down the cliff. With no room for the keepers' home next to the lighthouse, it was built at the top of the cliff. This necessitated the construction of a room next to the lighthouse for off-duty keepers who could not get up the cliff due to inclement weather. Weather added challenges, described in a newspaper article cited in National Park Service Historian Dewey Livingston's comprehensive history of the lighthouse:

> *Time and again, it is said, the workmen engaged in the construction of the buildings had their tools blown away, and once the breeze lifted bodily a carpenter's kit and*

hurled it over the cliff. A stiffish gale unroofed the keep-
er's house soon after its completion.

Despite the challenges, by August 1870, a fine keepers' home was finished, complete with a brick cellar, three coats of paint, and whitewashed outbuildings. Its first keeper, John Bull, and his wife, Melissa, moved in to prepare for the long-awaited completion of the lighthouse.

A San Francisco machinist, **Joseph Bien,** was given the contract to construct the tower and install the lighting apparatus. As he was the only one in California qualified to construct light towers according to government specifications, he was well paid for his work at a rate of 18 cents a pound. While the tower was being built, the first order three-ton Fresnel lens, consisting of thousands of pieces of hand carved glass curved to focus the weak light of the oil lamps into powerful rays that could be seen 24 miles out to sea, was being manufactured in France. These precious pieces of glass were then loaded on a ship bound for California. Once in San Francisco, they were loaded into an oxcart and hauled over rough roads to Point Reyes. When they arrived, one case of prisms was missing, spurring a frantic two-month search. Eventually, the case was found and, by December 1, 1870, the light began flashing its white beam every five seconds. This light, using four oil-burning wicks, required constant maintenance. Nevertheless, it was amazingly dependable, and shone flawlessly for 105 years until it was automated in 1975.

Despite the dependability of its light, many ships still wrecked at the point. Although its mid-cliff location was the wisest choice, heavy fogs still frequently blanketed the light. To warn ships during these heavy fogs, a coal-fired, steam-powered foghorn was installed. By June 1871, it began emitting its monotonous warning blasts. Unlike the light, this fog signal was plagued with problems and became the source of most of the keepers' frustrations. It was quirky and dangerous. It burned during its first spring of operation, silencing the foghorn, damaging a building, and requiring $10,000 in repairs.

Even when it was not catching fire, it required a great deal of maintenance, for it needed enormous amounts of two scarce resources, coal and water, to function effectively. Using 140 pounds of coal an hour, it consumed 42 tons of coal in 1875, all of which had to be hauled to the point and then carried down the cliff a full 100 feet beyond the light tower. It also required a great amount of water, a scarce commodity, for the lighthouse had been built in an area that received only 22 inches of rain per year. A constant problem, generations of keepers were forced to design water-saving solutions to satisfy their thirsty foghorn, as evidenced by the elaborate water catchment system that still remains. In addition to the hard work maintaining the foghorn, keepers dammed its unrelenting noise, described in this 1887 account in the *San Francisco Chronicle*:

> . . . the blast alone, which lasts five seconds and recurs every seventy seconds, is enough to drive any ordinary man mad, and must, it seems, exert a wearing effect upon even the hardened nerves of a keeper.

Despite the voracious appetite of the annoying foghorn, keepers were consistently plagued by complaints from ship captains who lamented that they could not hear the fog signal. As a result, there was constant experimentation to find a fog signal that would be less difficult to maintain and more audible to ship captains. By 1880, sirens had replaced the coal-driven signal and, by 1890, two half-inch whistles had replaced the sirens.

Life at the Lighthouse

The Point Reyes Lighthouse staff consisted of the Principal Keeper and three subordinates, called the First, Second and Third Assistants. All lived at the lighthouse residence and, until the Coast Guard took over its operation, were encouraged to bring their families. In 1887, pay was $800 a year for the Principal Keeper, $600 for the First Assistant, and $500 for Second and Third Assistants. In addition to their free housing, they were given rations, although there were ongoing complaints about their adequacy.

Supplies, also, were scarce and Principal Keepers were held

Polishing the Light's Fresnel Lens

responsible for maintaining a close watch on their usage. A February 24, 1937 letter from the Superintendent of Lighthouses, currently held in the National Seashore Archives, testifies to this scarcity with a yearly allocation of:

```
coal . . . . . . . . 6¾ tons
kerosene. . . . . 50 gallons
toilet paper. . . 12 rolls, 1 per month
saniflush. . . . . 3 cans, 1 every four months
matches. . . . . 48 boxes, 4 per month
```

The light shone from sunset to sunrise. Clockworks turned the giant Fresnel lens with a counterweight that completed its fall every four hours, necessitating four-hour shifts for keepers that began a half-hour before sundown and continued until the sun rose. On foggy nights, two keepers kept watch throughout the night, one in the light tower and the other at the fog signal below. During gales, it was often impossible for keepers to climb the steep cliff to the residence, and it was not uncommon for off-duty staff to sleep in the small room near the tower until the storm abated.

Tedious tasks, such as polishing the lens, maintaining the facility, and replenishing supplies by journeying either down to the sea landing or overland to town, consumed the daylight hours of keepers. The tedium was broken by friendships with local ranchers and recreational excursions to Olema or Point Reyes Station. The tedium was also broken occasionally by a heroic rescue, such as that of three crewmen of a fishing vessel stranded for 24 hours on a rocky cliff below the lighthouse. When the Drakes Bay Lifeboat Station staff was unable to reach them, Keeper Fred Kreth climbed down the 300-foot cliff and guided them to safety.

During much of its first 50 years, the Point Reyes Lighthouse was considered to be the least desirable assignment on the West Coast. Stifling loneliness plagued the staff. The nearest towns, Olema and, later, Point Reyes Station, offered little and were a full hour away over rough roads blocked by many gates that needed to be opened and then closed immediately. Although this isolation was not an unusual component of lighthouse duty, the addition of its ferocious weather, annoying fog signal, and treacherous journey down the cliff to the light soon made it a most unpopular assignment.

As a result, Point Reyes Lighthouse was plagued with more than its share of personnel problems, including insanity, alcoholism, violence, insubordination, and a constantly-changing staff. Logs record staff members who were verbally abusive and others who refused to maintain the fog signal, disappeared, missed their watch duty, and returned drunk. Additionally, turnover was high. During these frequent personnel changes, lighthouse operation and maintenance was clearly unsatisfactory. When one keeper, John C. Ryan, arrived in January 1888, he was appalled by its condition and noted that ". . . it is broken, filthy and almost a total wreck." The Third Assistant agreed with his assessment and wrote "Rats" over the entire entry. Focused on improving conditions, Ryan required more work from his assistants. Although the facilities improved under his leadership, some wonder if he demanded too much. According to the log of January 30, 1889, an assistant had a nervous breakdown: "The second assistant went crazy and was handed over to the constable at Olema." Ryan was dismissed soon afterward.

It was only during its last 50 years, when roads had been improved and modern conveniences, such as electricity, had reached it, that conditions improved and its undesirable reputation waned. Despite these problems, many recognized the invaluable service keepers provided, poetically expressed by the 1880 *History of Marin County:*

> *In the lonely watches of the dreary, stormy night, with the fury of the wind about him, with the roar and rush of the breakers dashing against the rocks below him, sounding in his ears, with no human soul near him, sits the keeper, true to his trust, faithful to his charge, doing well and honestly his duty, keeping the lamp trimmed and burning sending forth the ray to guide and make glad the storm-encircled sailor.*

The Point Reyes Lighthouse was placed under the authority of the United States Coast Guard (USCG) in 1939. It was not until 1951, when the last Lighthouse Service keeper, Gustav Zetterquist, retired, that Coast Guardsmen began staffing it. On June 12, 1975, the last USCG keeper, Thomas Smith, turned off the light after 105 years of constant service, replaced by the automated system in use today. When lighthouses throughout the United States were automated, their clockworks were often discarded. Point Reyes

Lighthouse was unique, for its clockworks were left intact, probably because its mid-cliff location made their removal, either by dragging them up the hill or tossing them over the cliff, too difficult.

Although the Coast Guard continues to operate the automated light and foghorn, the National Park Service now owns the lighthouse buildings and its adjacent 83 acres. Listed in the National Register of Historic Places, it is open to the public. Thousands visit each year to tour this extraordinary lighthouse, the only one in the nation retaining its original first order Fresnel lens plus its extremely rare, intact, operational clockworks. Many winter visitors are also enchanted by a spectacular view of the annual whale migration—for the lighthouse offers one of the coast's premier viewing spots.

Some visit on stunningly clear days and wish they could stay, romantically longing to turn back time and become one if its keepers. Fewer come when the winds are raging, furious waves crash below, and rain limits visibility to a few feet. Though they may not long to stay, it is these visitors who can share, for a moment, the grueling life of those who lived at the Point Reyes Lighthouse guiding mariners to safety.

Life-Saving Station

Despite the light and fog signal, many ships were still wrecked on the treacherous coastline. The relatively small number of lives that were lost is a testimony to the effectiveness of the lifesaving teams stationed nearby. Charged with the responsibility of rescuing seamen, a team of lifesavers was stationed on Point Reyes Beach in 1890. Subsequent teams served there and at the relocated station on Drakes Beach for almost a century. It was these courageous men who saved hundreds of crewmen and passengers from death in the raging seas.

Even before these lifesavers arrived, Point Reyes had a tradition of rescues, for ranchers often helped haul shipwrecked crew and passengers to safety. One of the more spectacular of these rescues was in 1861 when Carlisle Abbott heroically lassoed the crewmembers of the wrecked *Sea Nymph*. Several men, including its captain, left their vessel and attempted to reach the shore in a small boat. While ranchers watched from shore, it capsized in the surf. Immediately, Abbott, sprang into action. He loosened several ropes from the saddles of nearby horses, knotted them together, tied one end to his waist, handed the other end to a spectator, and dove into the breakers, grasping another long rope in his hand. According to the 1880 *History of Marin County*:

> With a skilled twirl of the rope in mid air he sent it with unerring aim over the captain's head, and in a trice had dragged him safely on shore. This was repeated until all the men were saved.

Despite the courage and creativity of ranchers like Abbott, it was soon clear that a lifesaving station was needed at Point Reyes. The first lifesaving station, built at Bolinas Bay in 1881, was short-lived. The sandbar at the mouth of the lagoon compromised its utility, for lifeboats

Launching a Lifeboat from the Station

could not get over it during low tide. When it burned six years later, it was not rebuilt for, by 1886, a new lifesaving station had been authorized on Point Reyes Beach, three miles north of the lighthouse. Although Charles Howard eventually donated the land, negotiations with him stalled the project. According to Lifesaving Assistant Inspector C. H. McLellan, Charles kept changing his mind, causing:

> *a great deal of trouble and vexatious delays. . . . Several times I considered the business satisfactorily settled, when after thinking of the matter over night, Mr. Howard whould [sic] change his mind and the work would have to be repeated.*

Finally, on January 20, 1888, agreement was reached and most believed that construction could begin. They were wrong. An unexpected difficulty arose when Charles refused to give the contractor access to the building site unless his tenants were given use of the telegraph at the station, a promise Charles insisted he had received verbally. After additional negotiations, an agreement was reached, and construction, bid at $8195, began in May 1889.

Not surprisingly, construction on the rough, exposed shore brought its own set of difficulties, not unlike the challenges of building the lighthouse. Heavy surf and high winds, unbroken by any vegetation or natural windbreaks, slowed work, while a three-week bout of dense fog stopped construction entirely. Additionally, roads needed more grading than expected, and the 20 miles to town made getting supplies challenging. An unexpected expense was incurred when an additional $292 was needed for a redwood picket fence to keep the cattle out.

Finally, on August 20, 1889, the boathouse and home for the Life-Saving Station surfmen was completed, and local dairyman, Henry Boesen, was hired as a caretaker. He was paid $40 a month and occupied the station until permanent staff arrived in April 1890 to begin operations. Although most lifesaving stations were staffed by eight surfmen and a keeper, the Point Reyes Station only needed seven staff: six surfmen to man the lifeboats and the keeper to steer. All seven arrived in July. Unfortunately, three left immediately, dissatisfied with conditions.

Although records do not specify these unsatisfactory conditions, they were probably based on the isolation and danger of the assignment. Although the isolation was daunting, the discomforts and dangers of the assignment were even more discouraging. Most soon grew to dread routine patrols on rough beaches in winds that could reach 100 miles an hour. Even those who did not dread the rough conditions were dissatisfied by their tediousness, for they almost never saw anything to report on these patrols. In addition to beach patrols, surfmen were required to launch the lifeboat twice a week. This practice required pushing the lifeboat through the dangerous surf, often strong enough to crush it, and rowing out to sea. During the Life-Saving Station's first three years of operation, three were killed in these routine drills, a chilling reminder of the Life-Saving motto: "Ye have to go out, but ye don't have to come in."

In addition to the lifeboat, the Life-Saving Station's most important piece of beach rescue equipment was its breeches buoy, a life ring attached to oversized trousers designed to carry stranded crew and passengers from a foundering ship to shore. It was deployed by firing a line to the mast of the wrecked ship using a miniature cannon

Breeches Buoy Rescue from the *Somoa*

called a Lyle gun, while the other end was secured on the beach. As soon as the breeches buoy, holding the stranded individual, was attached to this line, it was hauled ashore. A remarkably effective rescue device, its use was far more pleasant when conditions allowed the line to be secured high enough on that mast so that the occupant of the breeches was not dragged through the surf and over the rocks on the trip to shore.

On January 28, 1913, the Point Reyes Station launched what is remembered as the most effective breeches buoy rescue in history. The steamer *Samoa* was loaded with lumber for San Francisco when she ran aground at Point Reyes Beach in heavy fog. According to the logbook of Surfman Christopher Hunt:

> *We worked under great difficulties: that no one was lost or seriously injured by the mess of drifting lumber and heavy timbers that was [sic] thrown up by the rough sea is due to a great extent to the valuable assistance rendered us by the farmers and there [sic] hired help hauling the breeches buoy to and from the wreck. It enabled me to have two and three surfmen in readiness to run out into the surf and protect the shipwrecked man in the breeches buoy from being hit by flying lumber.*

Trying to Save the *Samoa*

Although the rescue of the **Samoa** is remembered as an extraordinarily successful one, Point Reyes Life-Saving Station's crew participated in many other amazing rescues. Although many changes took place during its 37 years of operation, including incorporation into the Coast Guard in 1915, its mission to rescue those on endangered ships never wavered. During these years, the passengers and crews from many wrecks, including six schooners, one brig, one bark, and six steamers, owe their lives to the tenacity and bravery of the station's crew.

Radio Breakthroughs

While Point Reyes' treacherous coast was gaining renown for its tragic shipwrecks, its important role in long distance communications enabled the rescue of countless passengers from disabled ships at sea. For over eight decades, its stations were among the world's most powerful radio facilities. Point Reyes' central role in radio history began when **Guglielmo Marconi** selected it for two of his stations in the first global wireless system. Marconi, an avid experimenter and astute businessman, creatively combined a number of inventions to be the first to successfully send wireless messages over long distances. In 1901, when he received a message sent 2000 miles from Cornwall, England to St. Johns, Newfoundland, he proved that wireless signals could travel long distances despite the curvature of the earth. This successful transmission witnessed the birth of the radio era.

Rejected when he offered his discovery to his native country, Italy, Marconi established companies in Britain and America. He quickly built high-powered transmitters throughout the world, creating the world's first practical, commercially-viable wireless system. By 1910, hundreds of ships maintained communication with land stations, an ability that is credited with saving thousands of lives. Its importance was clearly illustrated when Marconi met the rescue ship, *Carpathia*, and was greeted by *Titanic* survivors with the emotional cry, "We owe our lives to you."

Seeking the most interference-free location near San Francisco, by 1913 Marconi had purchased 643 acres of pastureland in Bolinas for a transmitting station, plus over a thousand acres on the east side of Tomales Bay near Marshall for a receiving and operating station. With the completion of these stations in 1914, Point Reyes was transformed into an internationally-important radio center. In 1916, these stations received messages from Papeete, Tahiti, 4000 miles away and Japan, an impressive 5400 miles away, in addition to unexpectedly intercepting German transmissions sent from stations over 7000 miles away.

When the United States entered World War I in 1917, all private wireless stations were confiscated. When the war ended in 1918, the Navy paid Marconi $789,500 for 45 of the coastal stations they had taken. He was allowed to retain some stations, including those at Point Reyes. Despite these reparations, post-war fears of foreign ownership fueled a move to exclude Marconi from the American wireless industry. By 1920, these efforts were successful. Marconi's American company was dissolved when General Electric paid $3.5 million for its controlling shares and established the Radio Corporation of America (RCA) in its place.

RCA soon emerged as America's wireless monopoly, installing the latest technology at Point Reyes and embarking on expansions that resulted in an enlarged Bolinas station and a new receiving station on the coast that would eventually replace the Marshall station. Seeking to buy the McClure Ranch for this new coastal station, RCA filed condemnation proceedings on it in 1929 when a satisfactory price could not be negotiated. A jury supported the condemnation but set its price at $127,000. Soon after this decision, construction began and, by 1931, a large new coastal station, complete with an Art Deco façade of fluted columns, was operating. These expanded stations, equipped with the newest technology, became, according to the *San Rafael Independent*:

> *. . . the nerve center of a vast radio communication system that will link the United States with all the important trans-Pacific countries from Australia north to Siberia.*

It was these facilities that witnessed many history-making transmissions and receptions, including news of Amelia Earhart's ill-fated flight, the bombing of Pearl Harbor, declaration of World War II, and critical communications during the Korean and Vietnamese conflicts.

Amazingly, the buildings of these pioneer radio stations have survived, many of which retain historic radio equipment. The Marshall station, reputed to have cost $226,000 in 1913, consists of an operations building, a large, 35-room hotel for staff and visitors, a powerhouse, two cottages, and various other buildings. Acquired by California State Parks in 1984, it is now a picturesque conference center.

In the 1970s, RCA sold most of the Point Reyes coastal station and all of its Bolinas property to the nonprofit Trust for Public Land who resold it to the federal government when land for the National Seashore was being acquired. Most of the Bolinas Transmitting Station, consisting of four buildings built by Marconi and three more built by RCA, and its surrounding land, is leased by the National Park Service to Commonweal, a nonprofit health research organization that has spent millions of dollars restoring the buildings. The National Seashore is currently cooperating with the Maritime Radio Historical Society to restore the Point Reyes coastal station with plans for a visitor center and renewed radio operations. These stations offer an invaluable view of radio history, yet another unique legacy offered by this extraordinary windswept peninsula.

Drakes Bay Lifeboat Station

In addition to the wireless technology that revolutionized communications, lifesaving changed dramatically in the early 20th century when heavy, 36-foot motorized lifeboats replaced rowed ones. Their adoption foretold the closure of the Point Reyes Life-Saving Station, one of many that were relocated to protected shores where larger stations with rail launch facilities could more easily be built.

In preparation for this change, land for a new station in Drakes Bay was purchased from the estate of Charles Howard in 1913. It took another 13 years before construction began. This time, delays were not due to land acquisition problems. Instead, it was the 1915 reorganization of lifesaving stations under the Coast Guard, followed by the outbreak of World War I, that delayed it. In the intervening years, the need for a new station intensified as dangerous conditions continued and a deteriorating facility further lowered the morale of the crew. By 1926, the Point Reyes Life-Saving Station was in desperate need of immediate renovation if not replacement. That year, Field Assistant Andre Fourchy pleaded to Washington:

> *Point Reyes is by far the worst station of the Pacific Coast, and from the standpoint of equipment and efficiency, it is practically nil ... In its present condition, the station is of no benefit whatever; either for lifesaving purposes, or for checking rumrunners.*

Finally, the new Drakes Bay Lifeboat Station was completed in 1927, and by late summer Officer-in-Charge **Howard Underhill** moved his family from their home in the storm-battered old station to their comfortable New England-style home in a far milder, protected location. In addition to the new home, the station was comprised of a pier, tracks for two boats, a boathouse, and several additional buildings. The buildings of the abandoned Life-Saving Station were sold to dairyman **Joseph Mendoza**, who moved them to his ranch.

Captain Howard Underhill

Initially busy with major rescues, an access conflict also dominated the early years of the lifeboat station. In 1919, the land surrounding the proposed station was sold to Mendoza. He built a fence with a locked gate to bar trespassers from hunting on his ranch or collecting abalone from the nearby beach. When the Drakes Bay Lifeboat Station was built, this fence blocked its access. Although Coast

Guardsmen were given keys to open the gate, they were routinely lost. In frustration, Coast Guard officials removed the lock, contending that the road to the station had been deeded to the government in 1869 when Charles Howard owned it.

In response, Mendoza hired a lawyer, and the lock returned to the gate. There was an uneasy peace until 1929, when Coast Guardsmen from Bolinas Lagoon arrived to help rescue the crew of the wrecked steamer *Hartwood*. They were locked out and had to dash to the Mendoza ranch house to get a key, delaying their arrival at the rescue scene by 30 minutes. After this incident, although the gate remained locked, tempers were taut, and frustrated Coast Guardsmen repeatedly cut off locks. It was not until 1940, a full 13 years after the establishment of the new station, that the lock was removed and replaced with a cattle guard.

The Drakes Bay Lifeboat Station was fully operational for 41 years until it was closed in 1968, replaced in 1963 by a more advanced facility at Bodega Bay. By 1969, its buildings were transferred to the National Park Service and were soon designated as National Historic Landmarks. Unique on the Pacific Coast as the only unaltered rail launching station, all of its principal structures and most of its secondary ones still stand, including the launchway, tracks, launching cradles, and one of its 36-foot lifeboats. Many who visit today marvel at its scenic location and simple buildings, imagining life as an idyllic retreat far from the stresses of congested cities. Only a few are able to imagine the travails of the Coast Guardsman living there in decades past, a life of loneliness, hardship, and danger.

Heroic Rescues

During its first nine years of operation, the Drakes Bay Lifeboat Station rescued crew and passengers from 45 wrecks and is credited with saving the lives of 280 individuals and more than $3 million in ships and cargoes. Only two months after the completion of the new station, a 72-foot fishing trawler, *Henrietta*, with a crew of three, caught fire off Point Reyes. Although the ship was a total loss, all crewmembers were saved. In 1929, surfmen rescued crew from their first large shipwreck, followed by amazing rescues each year for the next few years.

On the foggy, windy evening of June 27, 1929, the **Hartwood**, a 200-foot wooden steam schooner carrying lumber, went aground on the rocks. The Coast Guard received an SOS at 10:00 p.m. stating that the ship was taking on water and that its passengers, plus some of its crew, had been ordered to abandon ship. The station's motor-ized lifeboat was immediately deployed and soon sighted two lifeboats being tossed in the surf near the rocks. Lifeboat passengers included the captain's wife with their six-year old son and another seven-year old boy.

When all lifeboat passengers were aboard the now-overloaded Coast Guard boat and taken to safety, rescuers used one of the empty **Hartwood** lifeboats to the row to the foundering ship to rescue Captain Enstrom and the six seamen who had remained onboard. While the captain refused to leave the ship, breeches buoys were

USCG Lifeboat Station and Palidini Pier at Drakes Bay

rigged and four crewmen were dragged to safety through the ever-increasing swell. After making sure these men were safe, Guardsmen used the lifeboat to return again to the ship for the remaining two crewmen and the captain. Eventually, the Drakes Bay Guardsmen saved all 28 passengers and crew. They were aided by a steamer, *Admiral Peoples*, that stood by to relay messages, and, eventually, by the belated Bolinas Lagoon station crew who had been delayed by Mendoza's locked gate.

The owners sent a tug to try to free the ship. Too firmly lodged in rocks, the task was impossible, and the *Hartwood* was a total loss, with the exception of the compass, logbook, and nautical instruments that were salvaged by the Coast Guard. Salvage rights were purchased by an Inverness resident, **Elbert Reeves,** who removed and sold all that he, his family, and a small crew could salvage. Within six months, the *Hartwood* had broken up.

When the wreck was investigated, the captain admitted that he had ordered a premature course change and contended that the fog sirens had been inaudible and steel in the cargo had affected the compass. Whatever the reason, Captain Enstrom, an experienced veteran with over 200 Point Reyes passages, was found guilty of negligence and his license was suspended.

Less than a year later, near noon on May 8, 1930, a 250-foot, 3240-ton steel tanker, *Richfield*, hit a submerged reef about 500 yards off Chimney Rock at Drakes Bay. Carrying 25,000 barrels of gasoline (at 44 gallons each), it was one of the largest tankers operating along the West Coast at the time and the flagship of Richfield Oil of Los Angeles. Encountering a heavy fog and strong northwest current, Captain Henry Lee took a route close to the headlands to avoid the strong current and headwind. According to him, the ship was "literally picked up by a huge comber and lifted far inshore and dropped on the reef." Lifeboats were launched, and Captain Lee ordered his crew to abandon ship.

Coast Guardsmen immediately deployed their lifeboat to tow the vessel's lifeboats to safety and away from the rapidly growing oil slick. By afternoon, a tug had arrived to try to salvage the Richfield. It failed, and Captain Lee finally abandoned his ship when it was clear that it could not be saved. Although the ship was a total loss, 23,000 gallons of oil were saved when another tug arrived to pump it off the wrecked ship. Word of the disaster traveled fast and crowds gathered, hoping to see it explode. Station Captain Underhill eventually turned away the crowds by prohibiting parking because "the lawn around the station was being torn up by the hundreds of sightseeing cars." Elbert Reeves again purchased salvage rights, but high seas and the rapid break-up of the ship made it impossible for him to successfully salvage. During one of his unsuccessful attempts, all of his facial hair was scorched when the fumes in the ship exploded.

On November 7, 1931, the *Munleon*, a steel-hulled freighter carrying 800 tons of cargo, including sugar, radios, and cigarettes was on its way to Portland from Oakland when it encountered heavy fog. Captain Otto Hengst was asleep at the time. He had given Third Mate Chris Nielson orders to change course as soon as the Point Reyes Light had been passed. Nielson misjudged the ship's location. He believed the Point Reyes Lighthouse had been cleared and changed course too soon. The *Munleon* hit the Point Reyes Headland rocks at full speed, approximately 11 knots. Nielsen was injured when the force of the grounding threw him against the bridge, and sleeping crewmembers were tossed out of their bunks.

Soon after the lifesaving crew reached the ship, sea conditions wosened, and *Munleon's* lifeboats were deployed, carrying 25 crew. They were soon transferred to the larger Coast Guard lifeboat. The captain and two officers refused to leave. Early the next morning, the *Munleon* sank in approximately 16 feet of water. As it was sinking, Captain Hengst shot flares requesting help, and the Coast Guard rescued the remaining three men.

For just over a month, the sunken *Munleon* was pinioned on a sharp rock, again luring crowds to the station to watch the spectacle and wait for her to break up. As this crowd swelled to over 100, Mendoza began charging spectators 50 cents to cross his ranch to get to the station. When one of these spectators stole something from his

Munleon, Aground

ranch, Mendoza raised the fee to $1. On November 11, the Coast Guard held an open house for "the many visitors who wished to visit the station while they were near here viewing the wrecked *S. S. Munleon.*" Finally, a storm on December 27, 1931 broke her up.

Although these huge shipwrecks were not repeated yearly, Point Reyes storms continued to threaten vessels. On January 30, 1938, a storm brought 64-knot winds. These ferocious winds blew a fishing net overboard the 65-foot fishing trawler, *E Antoni,* where it got fouled in the propeller. The skipper's distress signals were observed at the station and lifesavers launched the lifeboat immediately, reaching *E Antoni* in about 10 minutes. While the raging seas and gale winds pushed the *E Antoni* and the lifeboat nearer and nearer to shore, waves broke over the lifeboat. Guardsmen on the lifeboat worked for over an hour trying to tow the trawler to safety. When the towline caught in the propeller of the lifeboat, they quickly deployed two large anchors to stop both ships from crashing into

85

the beach. Flares were lit to get more help from the station, but the fog was so heavy that they were not visible.

When these anchors dragged, the larger one had to be cut, and efforts to save the *E Antoni* ended. Instead, the Guardsmen loaded crewmembers into their lifeboat and began drifting toward shore, motor still disabled by the tow line caught in its propeller. As they were drifting to shore, they saw another crewmember on board, but it was impossible to return to the trawler. He jumped overboard, was tossed toward the shore, pulled from the surf by waiting Guardsmen, and revived. When everyone was safely on shore, they were taken to Mendoza's farmhouse for dry clothes and warm food.

Although all were saved, the Coast Guard suffered significant losses, for its lifeboat sustained an 11 by 3-foot gash in its hull, their largest anchor was lost, and other equipment was damaged. When the investigation concluded, the consensus was that the Coast Guardsmen used excellent judgment and deserved letters of commendation, which they got. Ranchers and local fishermen also praised the heroic crew, summed up by Lawrence "Lefty" Arndt:

> *All I can say is that if it wasn't for the Coast Guard, there would have been seven fishermen less around here.*

Not all wrecks at Point Reyes involved ships, and early in the morning of November 29, 1938, the lifeboat station crew found themselves rescuing victims of the crash of a United Airlines DC-3. After losing its bearings in a storm, it ran out of fuel. The captain shot flares and made an emergency sea landing about 1¼ miles west of the old Point Reyes Life-Saving Station. The plane stayed intact and drifted toward the rocks. Its four passengers and three crewmembers climbed through the door to the top of the plane and waited to be rescued.

The plane in distress was observed by the lighthouse keeper who informed the lifeboat station. Guardsmen tried to get to the plane but the steep, dangerous cliff made the wreck difficult to reach by land, and lifesavers in the water could see the plane, but not reach it. Although the plane's veteran pilot, Captain Charles Stead, warned them against it, three passengers and two crewmembers jumped off the plane and tried to swim ashore. One, stewardess Frona "Bobby" Clay, reached a rock but jumped back into the water when it looked as if the plane's broken wing was going to hit her. Captain Stead and the remaining passenger, Isadore Edelstein, a recently paroled convict, watched in horror as all five disappeared. Eventually, they also swam to shore and were pulled ashore and up the 400-foot cliff by lifesavers who had finally reached the area overland. Captain Stead was "hysterical," and Edelstein incapacitated by shock and exposure. More than a week after the crash, two bodies were found but the other three, including the stewardess who had reached shore but had jumped into the surf again, were never found.

The last major rescue by the Drakes Bay Lifeboat Station crew has been called "one of the most amazing mass rescues in maritime history." On May 31, 1944, the *Henry Bergh*, a 10,500-ton Liberty ship transporting 1300 soldiers home from duty in the South Pacific, hit a reef at the Farallon Islands, 20 miles southwest of Point Reyes.

Wreck of the United Airlines DC-3

Drakes Bay crew motored quickly to the ship, while the Bolinas Station crew was kept in the lagoon by a low tide, unable to participate in the rescue. Navy destroyers and Coast Guard cutters also sped to the rescue. By the time they arrived, hundreds of men were in the water, while hundreds of others waited on the ship. A rescue plan was quickly put into action, and 15 to 20 men at a time jumped into the Coast Guard lifeboat using safety netting. They were then quickly transported to a nearby destroyer or cutter. This was repeated over and over again until all had been rescued. Remembered as a flawless operation, all were saved and only two of the 1300 were even injured. One of the rescued men told a reporter that the whole rescue was "no different from a routine drill." The ship did not fare as well and broke into pieces the next day. Although Captain Joseph Chambers claimed that his navigation equipment was not working properly, he was charged with incompetence and negligence and lost his license for two years.

The amazing rescue of the passengers of the *Henry Bergh* was the last large-scale operation of the Drakes Bay Lifeboat Station. The widespread use of accurate navigational equipment decreased the number of large ships that foundered on the dangerous rocks of Point Reyes, and it was soon clear that the days of heroic lifesaving operations using lifeboats and breeches buoys had ended.

Staff at the lighthouse and both lifesaving stations experienced extreme weather, danger, and loneliness. Despite these hardships, many of these men remembered Point Reyes fondly for its incredible beauty, its dramatic storms, the friendliness of local ranching families, and the camaraderie born of isolation. They also recalled the rescues, savoring the satisfaction of well-executed operations and their roles as heroes. Mariners, though, continue to approach Point Reyes with trepidation, breathing a sigh of relief when they have safely passed its ferocious surf and deadly rocks. Although shipwrecks, dominating Point Reyes' coastal history for over four centuries, may have diminished in number, not a mariner today passes the peninsula without a chilling awareness of the many ships destroyed on its treacherous shore.

New Owners

Each of the purchasers of the Shafter-Howard dairy ranches had different reasons for acquiring them, and, consequently, their fates varied greatly. Despite these differences, most would agree that these new owners, whether it was Murphy, who struggled one step ahead of his creditors, or Rapp and David, who profited almost immediately, revitalized the area and brought new hope and vision to Point Reyes. With them came renovated facilities, improved operations, enhanced quality, and a new pride permeating the community.

John Rapp's Ownership

As soon as the court intervened and ordered Charles and Emma's children to divide the ranches they had inherited, each sold their portion to the wealthy San Franciscan, John Rapp, who immediately resold all but the Bear Valley Ranch for a large profit. In addition to netting himself a great deal of money, he was also able to implement his philosophy that ranchers should own the land they worked.

One prime example of this was the Mendoza family who, after leasing for years, was finally able to purchase their own ranch. Joseph Vierra Mendoza was born in the Azores in 1883 and immigrated to the United States when he was 16 years old. He initially worked for his uncle for room and board only, but began earning 50 cents a day when his passage had been paid. Before long, he became a butter maker at another Point Reyes ranch. By 1909, a decade after he arrived in the United States, he partnered with his brother-in-law to lease N Ranch from the Shafter estate. That year he also married a young girl, **Zena**, who had journeyed to Point Reyes from the Azores two years earlier at the age of 11. Three years later they had a daughter, Tessie, and a son, Joseph Hamilton, six years after that. Years later, in 1961, when Zena was testifying against the National Park acquisition of their ranch, she recalled those difficult days:

We had to work awfully hard, and they would not make any improvements in the place. Even the most necessary things, like nails and lumber, we had to pay for out of our own pockets. The only thing they did was to be sure that the rent would be there even before the time.

In 1919, the Mendozas purchased the A and B Ranches from John Rapp. Finally, after many years of working at others' dairies and a decade of leasing, they were landowners. As soon as he owned his ranches, Mendoza began making needed improvements,

Joseph and Zena Mendoza

even acquiring the abandoned structures from the original Life-Saving Station at Point Reyes Beach for additional outbuildings.

Although they had fulfilled their dream of becoming landowners, life was not easy. Taxes on the ranches were high, sometimes as much as $200 per month and the Mendozas struggled to improve their ranches, while clothing and feeding their young family. With no electricity, they depended on kerosene lamps, battery banks, and gasoline-driven cream separators. The only telephone service was one the ranchers installed and maintained themselves. Extremely isolated, Point Reyes Station was 18 miles of muddy roads away, requiring the opening and closing of 15 gates each way. Far from doctors and with young children to protect, Zena borrowed books from the local doctor and taught herself basic nursing and first aid. Schooling was also a challenge, and the Mendozas hired a teacher to educate their children.

Improvements came slowly. By the mid-1920s roads were improved but they had to wait until 1939 for electricity. During the Depression, when milk prices plummeted, they rented some of their land to farmers who grew artichokes and peas. By 1941, when prices rebounded, they began shipping milk and cream again. That same year, Mendoza turned the operation of the ranches over to his son, Joseph Hamilton, who had just graduated from the University of California, Davis with a degree in agriculture.

Joseph Mendoza died in 1950. In 1961, his widow, Zena, was swept into the national spotlight by her passionate plea against National Park Service acquisition. When the Park Service purchased their land, they negotiated a renewable lease, and family members today run a modern, Grade A dairy, complete with electronic milking machines and computers that calculate production and control feeding. Successful dairy ranchers, after years of laboring and leasing land from others, the Mendozas characterize many ranchers who were able to finally purchase their ranches.

Although Rapp sold most of the ranches quickly, he kept Bear Valley Ranch. He hired a manager and invested enough to transform it into one of Marin County's finest certified dairies. Due to its reputation for quality and cleanliness, it was awarded contracts with San Francisco hospitals and its finest restaurants. In 1923, he built an expensive country home, reputed to have cost $12,000, overlooking Bear Valley. He also dammed a creek to make a lake for swimming and boating. He, his three daughters, and his son spent summers there enjoying horseback riding, swimming, hunting, and hiking.

On September 1, 1925, Rapp traded his ranch to **Colonel Jesse Langdon** for shares in a hardware business. The colonel continued to improve the ranch and got the best milkers by paying $90 a month, approximately 3 times the local wage. By 1928, Bear Valley's 500 cows, considered to be one of the state's largest disease-free herds, were producing 700 gallons of milk a day. Despite this success, he was not a popular owner, for he was both a dour disciplinarian and a compulsive perfectionist. During the Depression, his dairy lost its prestigious certification, and, as a result, his contracts with San Francisco hospitals were cancelled. Without these contracts, the colonel could not pay his $212,000 mortgage, and he lost the dairy. The bank bought it at auction for $125,000 and immediately offered it for sale. The Langdons were evicted in 1943 when **Eugene Compton**, a wealthy cafeteria owner, took possession.

Compton spent money to improve the ranch, constructing a number of new buildings, including a home, hay barn, meat house, horse barn, garage, and equipment shop. He also brought back the energy and goodwill that had been lost during Langdon's years, largely by the three rodeos he hosted in 1946, '47, and '48. He entertained locals, attracted rodeo competitors from across the state, and supported worthy causes, as he donated all the money generated. The community was saddened when he sold the ranch only six years later to Grace Kelham, heiress to the Spreckels sugar fortune, and her husband. Uninterested in dairying, they sold the herd, auctioned the equipment and began running beef cattle instead.

Leland Murphy's Ownership

When real estate developer Leland Murphy purchased Julia's ranches, he embarked on a journey of hope and heartbreak. Having just sold an orange grove in Ventura County, Murphy had money and was targeted as a good prospective purchaser. He was taken to Point Reyes to hunt quail and ended up falling in love with its wild beauty. Initially blinded by its stunning scenery, it was not long before he faced some harsh realities. His nine dairies, each with about 100 head of cattle, generated barely enough to cover taxes. Even more disturbing were the rotting cattle carcasses that dotted his land. Horrified, he rode from ranch to ranch asking why they had died. He learned that many had sickened from tuberculosis and that even the healthy ones could not be found, for they wandered freely from ranch to ranch over fences that had fallen into disrepair.

It was soon clear that his dairy ranches were not functioning well enough to generate even the modest rent payments. It was not long before he discovered his tenants' real source of income. Leland learned that his tenants were rumrunners when Red Lavazzoli's wagon full of artichokes got stuck in the mud. To free it, he was forced to unload his artichokes, revealing thousands of dollars worth of Scotch whiskey in sacks under the floorboards. Leland knew that he would fail if he tried to stop this lucrative smuggling. Instead, he concentrated on improving the ranches to produce a profit again. His first project was to re-fence them. When the railroad ceased operation along Tomales Bay, he was able to purchase 10,000 narrow gauge ties for 10 cents each. When split, they made perfect fence posts, and he soon began his daunting fencing project.

Unfortunately, 1933 brought new challenges. When Prohibition was repealed, smuggling ended, and his tenants left. Almost overnight, Leland was left with 10,550 unproductive acres and a looming debt. Instead of trying to rebuild all his diaries, he concentrated on rebuilding the Home Ranch and sought other uses for the rest of his ranches. He sold most of his cows. At first, he replaced them with sows, but decided that his magnificent land deserved better than the snorting, smelly animals. He tried raising chickens, beef cattle, and cultivating barley, oats, and hay.

Additionally, he leased land to Japanese tenants who planted peas. Although Point Reyes eventually became the world's foggiest pea patch, the first year of growing peas was disastrous. With high hopes, Murphy paid for the seed peas and bought tractors. Only a few days before harvest, the crop withered and was lost. Facing increased pressure from the bank, Leland took the bank officer on a quail hunt and was able to convince him to extend the loan. Eventually, he had five successful pea farms, and healthy pea plants covered the land that had been California's finest pastureland. In addition to these pea farms, Leland's land began to produce some of California's finest vegetables, including artichokes grown by Italian tenants that were considered to be the best in the state.

With thriving pea and artichoke farms, the future looked bright for Leland. Unfortunately, just as he was beginning to see some profits, the United State entered World War II. His Japanese pea farmers were sent to internment camps, while the Italian artichoke farmers were moved to safety camps. Leland was again faced with unproductive land. After the war, Mexican tenants revitalized the pea farms, while artichoke farming ceased when it became evident that its deep furrows had caused erosion damage.

Although Leland never lived there, he came as often as possible, frequently hosting large barbecues and hunting and fishing excursions for his San Francisco friends. Although he lost one ranch through a foreclosure and had to sell 4 other ranches at low prices in the 1940s, Leland still owned 3013 acres when the National Park Service acquired Point Reyes. By the 1960s, he had given his Point Reyes land to his son, Leland, Jr., who continued to raise beef cattle after the National Seashore acquired it in 1968.

Despite consistently looming debt, Leland loved his wild expanses of grassland and tenaciously held on to them. When local historian Jack Mason interviewed Murphy shortly before his death at the age of 87 in 1978, he said that the ranches had come as close to bankrupting him as they had Julia. "But I have no regrets, none at all. That's a grand place out there, and it was a privilege owning it as long as I did." Just after his death, Mason said of him: ". . . he is very much alive, as is Mrs. Hamilton; no one will ever give as much to the land, or take as little from it, as they."

Leonard David's Ownership

Like Rapp, **Leonard David** sold most of his land almost immediately at a large profit. Five of the ranches he purchased were sold within a week and the other two were sold within a year for an average of $50,000 each. Although these ranches were offered to tenants, none were sold to them, but were purchased, instead, by outsiders. These new owners immediately began improving them, most eventually achieving Grade A certification. In addition to his quick profit on the dairy ranches, Leonard sold some land for $20 an acre, traded other property for a Santa Barbara hotel valued at $80,000, and sold the timber rights on Inverness Ridge to the Sweet Lumber Company. On top of all these profits, he retained land on Tomales Bay with plans to develop a resort. Little more than a business opportunity for Leonard, he was able to profit immediately from the land that had been such a drain on the resources of Oscar and his heirs for so many decades.

Wartime Activities

As World War II raged in Europe, Point Reyes felt the shadow of war when Laguna Ranch was leased as a training camp for the United States 30th Infantry Division. Named Camp Heidel, tents were pitched for 500 men, and the training began. For awhile, soldiers lived comfortably next to Leland Murphy's Japanese pea farmers. Everything changed on December 7, 1941, when Pearl Harbor was attacked, and they found themselves escorting their hard-working neighbors to detention centers.

This Japanese attack brought a disturbing, but distant, war to the shores of Point Reyes, for many believed that Drakes Bay was vulnerable to a Japanese invasion. Before long, the peninsula had been converted to a defensive stronghold with bunkers and gun emplacements, while bluffs and beaches were continuously patrolled. The Army took possession of the eastern end of the lighthouse property. It installed utilities and constructed barracks, recreation facilities, and radio buildings, most of which were demolished in 1952. Troops were also stationed at Muddy Hollow Ranch, Olema, and near the Radio Corporation of America (RCA) transmission facility on the coast. Abbott's Lagoon became a bombing range. Additionally, the large mansion that had been built in 1914 by the International Order of Foresters (I.O.O.F.) at Point Reyes Station was converted into a hospital.

Olema's Nelson Hotel, family-run for over six decades, was converted into a barracks and the Nelsons were given two days to move, taking all their possessions. Soon after their eviction, Edgar Nelson, shot himself in the hotel yard. Although the Army had agreed to repair any damage, when it was given back to the Nelsons in 1944, the damage was extensive. Although the Nelsons eventually received $3,000 for their losses, the Nelson Hotel sank into disrepair until it was lovingly renovated in the 1980s and re-opened.

Residents who were not called up were kept busy preparing for attack and maintaining important wartime agricultural production. The Inverness Garden Club rolled "Bandages for Britain," and everyone endured shortages. Ranchers were especially challenged by the unavailability of the materials they needed. Amid this hard work, the dark side of patriotism surfaced when a Point Reyes rancher, German immigrant **Dr. Edward Heims**, was anonymously accused of hiding Nazi spies and German airplanes in his barn. As a result of these accusations, he was taken into custody and interrogated at a government facility in the Midwest. Although he was exonerated of all charges, the poisonous gossip had done its damage, and he remained isolated and alienated throughout the war.

Despite the upheaval they brought, residents welcomed soldiers enthusiastically. The USO came to entertain troops, and locals helped by serving soda and donuts, while proper, well-chaperoned girls danced with them. Some of the more adventurous soldiers gravitated to the stronger drink and freer girls at local bars, where they spent many memorable evenings drinking, gambling, and jitterbugging the night away.

After the War

Although the conclusion of the war brought enormous population surges to many coastal California towns, Point Reyes remained undiscovered and sparsely populated. Residents worked hard and enjoyed sailing, clamming, crabbing, and fishing on the bay; picnicking on the beach; and horseback riding through the magnificent undeveloped expanses of land. For an evening out, many enjoyed monthly square dances and ate complete lobster dinners offered for $5 at the Silver Dollar Restaurant.

The 1940s and 1950s did bring some unsettling changes. Small school districts were consolidated, and one-room schoolhouses were closed. The creamery also closed. Instead, oil companies came hoping to drill and a developer sold beachfront lots on Drakes Bay. Gradually, as word of the sparse simplicity and spellbinding beauty of Point Reyes began to spread, the whisper of change began to permeate the peninsula. This whisper became a roar in 1958, when the government announced its plans to turn Point Reyes into a National Seashore. Apprehension swept the area, for all knew that their way of life was about to end.

Connected to the Past; Eye to the Future

As early as 1935, the National Park Service (NPS) considered acquiring Point Reyes. When NPS planners were asked to identify potential shoreline parks, they enthusiastically ranked Point Reyes among their top choices, recommending the purchase of 53,000 acres at Point Reyes for $2.4 million ($45 per acre). Although in hindsight, this was a bargain, the NPS rejected this option in favor of other locations that offered sunny and warm summers. Thus, except for small county parks that were gradually established, Point Reyes remained private and gated for the next few decades.

Eventually, plans for the housing development at Drakes Bay took shape. The Sweet Lumber Company began logging the hundreds of acres of timber rights it had purchased from Leonard David, and the sawmill near Five Brooks in Olema Valley swung into action. Additionally, other subdivisions were proposed, and there was discussion of a freeway to the coast. The Marin County Board of Supervisors, often split 3 to 2, supported these development plans and approved a growing number of permit applications. The peninsula was clearly on the verge of becoming another busy suburb. The testimony of one rancher summed it up when he said that, by the year 2000,

> ... there will no longer be a Marin County. There will be a greater city of San Francisco. ... The section we have under discussion today [Point Reyes], gentlemen, will be as intensely built over as Palo Alto or Burlingame or San Mateo.

Shocking Announcement

Aware of the unalterable changes that were about to occur at Point Reyes, the 1956 NPS study of possible seashore parks again recommended its acquisition. This time, NPS Planning Chief George Collins was so worried about the looming development that he used his own money to print a report recommending the immediate acquisition of 35,000 acres at Point Reyes. When his report was released in 1958, shock waves reverberated throughout the peninsula. Bay Area newspaper headlines heralded the news that NPS would ask Congress for approval, condemning as many as 24 ranches to acquire the land.

Ranchers sprang into action in opposition. Although the NPS plan to acquire Point Reyes was applauded by some who saw it as the only way to protect the peninsula from development, most locals opposed it. Years of impassioned debate ensued. Pro-acquisition conservationists had the powerful political backing of U.S. Congressman Clem Miller, and California's U.S. Senator Clair Engle. Opposition came from a well-organized group of locals composed of ranchers, RCA, the Chamber of Commerce, Marin County Board of Supervisors, and, of course, landowners with development plans.

No!

Shortly before she died in 1936, Julia Shafter Hamilton said, "Some day . . . the government is going to take that land. . . . and give it to the people." With her words echoing in their ears, ranchers gathered to fight NPS acquisition and hired a lawyer, Bryan McCarthy, to represent them. By late March 1961, Congressional hearings concerning the acquisition were held in Washington, D.C. Although many testified, it was Zena Mendoza's emotional plea, a portion of which follows, that most effectively captured the feelings of the ranchers who fought the NPS acquisition:

> [Point Reyes] is where my children were born . . . and my grandchildren were raised. . . . Now I am faced with the possibility of losing everything that I have worked for. The strangest thing is that I was never approached. Everything was done underhanded. . . . Nobody ever came to me to ask, 'Do you want to sell your property for a

park?'. . . If my ranches would be taken for defense, well, you have to sacrifice, but it is for the benefit of all, for the benefit of my family as well as for the others. But for recreation, what kind of recreation did I have when I was a youngster? Work and save so my children would have a sense of security and heritage that I felt belonged to them. Now every inch of my land is supposed to disappear.

Ranchers described their critical role providing food while also preserving and protecting Point Reyes from development. They contended that, while the land was extremely valuable as ranchland, its dangerous beaches and cold, foggy summers would make it undesirable as a park. They warned of the catastrophic impact on the rich wildlife when visitors flooded the area and predicted the migration of deer, the ruin of oyster beds, and the death of abalone. They also lamented the increased smog these visitors would inevitably bring to their beloved peninsula. On a fiscal note, they predicted that, in light of escalating land values, the NPS did not have enough budgeted to buy their ranches. Strongly supported by both the local Chamber of Commerce and County Supervisors, they also warned of the tax shortfall that would result when their ranches were removed from the tax rolls, a shortfall that would hurt other Marin County landowners.

Basing their opposition on the importance of Point Reyes as agricultural land and their rights as private landowners, locals staged a strong, well-organized, and well-articulated opposition. Describing the NPS acquisition of Point Reyes as the government's tyrannical attempt to grab their land, Bryan McCarthy summed up their argument well when he stated, "The Interior Department has never before gone into an area and destroyed an industry, and that is what they are doing."

Yes!

Opposing them were equally strong conservation forces, buttressed by the enthusiastic support of some powerful politicians. They contended that the spectacular peninsula should belong to all and would provide the perfect escape for city-dwellers weary of urban congestion. As did the ranchers, they based much of their argument on the need to protect Point Reyes' unique wildlife, insects, and plants. While the ranchers described themselves as protectors of the land, pro-park advocates criticized them for using pesticides and fertilizers, some even accusing them of shooting golden eagles during lambing season. The most radical of this group demanded the cessation of all ranching on the peninsula.

In addition to these environmental issues, park advocates predicted that property values would increase if the National Seashore were established, increasing the tax base rather than decreasing it, as opponents had charged. They also contended that local businesses would profit from the influx of tourists, again increasing county revenues. An impassioned plea by Joel Gustafson, Board President of the Point Reyes National Seashore Foundation, summarized the hopes and fears for the peninsula so loved by opponents and advocates alike: "The nation can have an area that would be invaluable for public enjoyment . . . or we can by default let this jewel be carved by the bulldozer and smeared over by asphalt."

Supporters of NPS acquisition were helped by their powerful political advocates. Newly-elected U.S. **Congressman Clem Miller** from Inverness knew the area well and actively supported the establishment of a National Seashore by partnering with NPS Planning Chief Collins and local conservation groups. When this group was joined by U.S. **Senator Clair Engle,** the tide began to turn. While Engle lobbied the Senate, Miller advocated its approval in the House of Representatives. He also masterminded the recall of the leading anti-park county supervisor, followed by the election of a pro-park replacement. Nature cooperated, for each time they brought guests to visit the peninsula, the weather was perfect—warm and bright—leading guests to conclude that warnings about its unappealing weather were exaggerated. Soon after **President John F. Kennedy** took office in 1961, he and his Secretary of the Interior Stewart Udall declared the acquisition of Point Reyes a priority. Discussions soon turned from "If" to "How?" and "How big?"

Compromise

Early in the debate, the Marin Conservation League began negotiating to preserve dairying in the area. They advocated coexistence, stating that the combination of park activities and dairying was the perfect use of the land. They envisioned a landscape, untouched by developers' bulldozers, but dotted with picturesque 1870s ranches and cows grazing on the hills. Advocating ranch leasebacks, they forwarded a proposal supporting the NPS purchase of the entire peninsula, followed by the lease of portions to selected ranchers and other desirable business owners. Many ranchers had previously been tenants and were adamantly opposed to becoming tenants again.

Despite their concerns, as ranchers realized they would lose their battle to keep their land, they began to seriously consider this leasing option. When respected ranchers such as Boyd Stewart of the Olema Valley Stewart Ranch and Joseph Hamilton Mendoza, owner of an 8000-acre dairy empire, began to support leasing, others saw its advantages, and negotiations for leasebacks were initiated. Although price was a prime consideration, another important area of negotiation concerned promises that tourists would not interfere with ranch operations. Negotiations were further complicated by the government's indecision over how much land it wanted to acquire.

Mutually agreeable conditions were hammered out, and the Mendozas were among the first to agree to leaseback provisions, including a selling price of approximately $800 an acre and renewable leases. Eventually, approximately 18,000 acres were sold and leased back for ranching. Today, Mendoza says, "It has been a good partnership." And, most ranchers agree with him.

Despite a good working partnership, life at a National Seashore has its challenges. Like other independently-owned California dairies, Point Reyes ranchers face intense competition from large dairy corporations, in addition to expensive regulatory mandates. Added to these concerns, Point Reyes dairymen must work within the complex structure of a large federal agency, making dairying at Point Reyes complex and fraught with unexpected challenges.

A Park is Born

Congress approved the Point Reyes National Seashore, and it became law when, on September 13, 1962, President Kennedy signed the bill authorizing the acquisition of 53,000 acres and allocating $13 million. Most credit three men, Congressman Clem Miller, Senator Clair Engle, and a sympathetic President Kennedy with the establishment of the park. Had the timing been different, it is likely that it would never have been established. Within two years, all three of these men had died. Only three weeks after the bill was signed, Miller died in an air crash. Engle died of cancer in 1964. Kennedy was assassinated in 1963, reportedly planning a trip to dedicate the Point Reyes National Seashore when he changed his itinerary to include his tragic visit to Dallas.

As soon as the National Seashore was authorized, the NPS moved quickly to stop the development threatening it. Although Drakes Bay Estates were well underway with 18 homes completed, the NPS successfully stopped construction and removed all but three of the completed homes. Logging on Inverness Ridge was also stopped when the NPS acquired the Sweet Lumber Company's timber rights. In 1963, the NPS paid $5,725,000 to purchase Bear Valley Ranch for their headquarters, placing them near the site of the hacienda Garcia had built over a century earlier.

Despite these successes, it soon became clear that acquisition of the land would not be easy. In fact, it has been cited as an illustration of how not to buy a park. With the exception of Cape Cod National Seashore, authorized only a year earlier, all National Parks had been created from land already owned by the government. At Point Reyes, NPS officials had neither experience nor guidelines to assess the worth of the land, and worked with multiple independent appraisals that fluctuated from $40 an acre to $5000 an acre. In addition to price discrepancies, the NPS was unprepared to negotiate effectively with unwilling buyers. As a result, by 1965, all the money had been spent, and NPS owned less than half of the land it needed to create the park. Additionally, what it owned was scattered in small, unusable portions. With land values escalating and developers competing to buy the same land, NPS was forced to ask for more money. Initially Congress agreed to an additional allocation, but, in 1969, before this extra money could be used, President Richard M. Nixon, in his efforts to economize, froze all Point Reyes allocations. Desperate, the NPS considered selling some of the outlying land it had just acquired so that more central tracts could be purchased.

Time was running out, and impatient landowners began selling to developers. At Pierce Point, the northern tip of the peninsula, a community of 4500 homes was proposed, and bulldozers began grading for a development at Lake Ranch. In desperation, Marin conservation groups launched a "Save Our Seashore" initiative, presenting President Nixon with over 500,000 signatures asking for release of the money needed to establish the park. The initiative was successful and, by November 19, 1969, Nixon agreed to release the funds. Despite this success, the delays had been costly, and acquisition totaled $56 million, over 4 times the projected estimates. Finally, by September 16, 1972, the Point Reyes National Seashore was officially established by the Department of Interior.

Revised Visions

These delays, though worrisome and expensive, had one important outcome: Point Reyes, like Cape Cod National Seashore, had been acquired to serve a large metropolitan area. As such, it was initially conceptualized to accommodate recreational activities. To do this, plans were made to modify the landscape to serve large numbers of tourists and their dune buggies, motor boats, campers, trailers, and cars. With this in mind, a multi-lane Limantour road was authorized in 1966. Requiring much blasting and filling, locals and conservationists were appalled and filed a lawsuit to block its construction. Although the lawsuit was thrown out and construction began, luckily, the funding ran out before it was completed. Today, it remains unfinished, a three-and-one-half mile expressway from Seashore Headquarters west toward Limantour that abruptly changes to two narrow lanes near the summit, the single reminder of the highway-strewn park that could have been if funding had not been delayed.

By 1972, when the park was officially established, plans had changed. The passage of the 1964 Wilderness Act greatly influenced its development by shifting focus from recreational to wilderness uses. As a result, Point Reyes would remain as natural as possible, rescuing the majestic peninsula from a future filled with buzzing dune buggies and thundering caravans of motor homes.

Another reason Point Reyes developed differently in the 1970s than it would have in the 1960s was the establishment of the Golden Gate National Recreation Area. With its acquisition, Point Reyes became the northernmost portion of a vast and unique 100,000-acre park adjacent to San Francisco. Beginning in 1975, the NPS held over 200 meetings to determine the best uses for this amazing preserve. Although uses for Alcatraz sparked much controversy, most agreed that Point Reyes should be left untouched. Since then, it has not only remained undeveloped, but efforts have been made to allow areas to revert to their natural state. Initially proposed as 5000 acres of wilderness, in 1976, Congress designated 32,000 acres as wilderness, prohibiting permanent structures, major roads, and motorized vehicles, except for emergencies.

In addition to preserving the NPS land, these years saw efforts to preserve the land surrounding the park. In 1972, the Marin Board of Supervisors approved A-60 zoning for land not owned by NPS. This zoning required a minimum lot size of 60 acres, making it almost impossible for developers to create residential communities. In 1980, in a marriage between environmentalists and ranchers, the Marin Agricultural Land Trust (MALT) was established. This innovative organization buys development rights from ranch owners to ensure that the property remains agricultural, even if it is sold. It provides a classic win-win: ranchers get welcome cash and lower tax rates, while the community wins by retaining its agricultural land. MALT has already acquired the development rights for over 35,000 acres.

The funding delays generated anxiety for conservationists, NPS officials, and ranchers. The delays also resulted in far higher costs. Nevertheless, most would agree that the long wait smothered plans for a motorized playground, and, instead, allowed the natural magic of Point Reyes to survive, relatively untouched, by the 2 million people who visit it each year.

Evolving Towns

Initially a safe harbor for smugglers avoiding taxation and a timbering port, by the late 1960s, Bolinas had become home to a large community of idealistic hippies, many of whom had left San Francisco's Haight-Ashbury for a less populated paradise. In 1971, they succeeded in scrapping a master plan that called for a population of 28,000 by imposing a moratorium on new homes and defeating efforts to widen its access highway. Instead, a plan was approved that made agriculture, fishing, and small businesses the town's economic base. Bolinas soon gained renown for its unusual structures and recreational drug use, illustrating disregard for building codes and drug laws. Although those days are gone, Bolinas remains a charming, but totally unique, corner of this magnificent peninsula with some residents who continue to tear down road signs in hopes that tourists will not find it

Olema, virtually deserted when the railroad stopped at Point Reyes Station, languished until the 1960s when millions of visitors began coming to the adjacent National Seashore. Soon, a grocery store opened, the Catholic Church returned, and the Nelson Hotel was lovingly restored, reopening as the Olema Inn and Restaurant. Although still small, today's Olema offers a charming, slow-paced respite from the unchecked growth and congestion challenging many of California's coastal towns. Inverness remains a small community of charming cottages, lovely gardens, and uncongested streets amid a stunning setting. It exudes the aura of a village of yesteryear, populated with modern residents who are clearly aware of their good fortune to live there.

Building at Point Reyes Station began slowly after World War II. By 1954, a medical center, a school, and an impressive $40,000 shopping center, including a drugstore, dentist, coffee shop, and library, had been completed. The train station became the local post office, while the former engine house was converted into a community center. In the 1970s, hippies established cottage industries in abandoned homes and shops. At the same time, the Coast Guard bought 30 acres formerly used as railroad cattle pens. They used this land to build housing for the 36 families and 42 enlisted men that were affiliated with new radio installations at Point Reyes and Bolinas. Unlikely comrades, locals watched in amusement as their new military and peace-loving residents learned to co-exist. Continuing as a supply and service center for locals, it has also become a popular destination for visitors to the Point Reyes National Seashore who enjoy its leisurely pace, charming shops, fine restaurants, and extraordinary butter-filled pastries at the Bovine Bakery.

Although its four major towns, Bolinas, Olema, Inverness, and Point Reyes Station, changed gradually, each has slowly adapted to their peculiar circumstances. They have evolved steadily into the radically different communities they are today, each with a different role in the history and future of this wonderful peninsula.

Floods and Fire

Point Reyes remains vulnerable to the natural forces that have battered it throughout the centuries. Since it has been a National Seashore, it has experienced some extraordinary floods and the memorable Vision Fire of 1995. On January 3, 1982 storms deluged the peninsula with 12 inches of rain. Streams overflowed their banks, sweeping everything along, including houses, cars, bridges, and propane tanks. Mudslides tore out trees, blocked roads, disrupted water supplies, and tore down power lines. Six homes in Inverness were totally destroyed, while many others were severely damaged, and the small town was totally isolated for three days. Thankfully, no one was killed or badly injured. The following year had the wettest recorded winter and an enormous storm was followed by another damaging flood. This time Stinson Beach took the brunt of the damage when huge waves engulfed homes.

Accustomed to raging storms and floods, the 1995 Vision Fire shocked everyone by its swift progress and devastation. On October 3, it broke out near the summit of Mount Vision and raged through the bishop pine forests on Inverness Ridge. By October 4, it was consuming an acre every five seconds. More than 2000 firefighters from all over the state, more than half of whom were inmates from correctional institutions, fought the fire. Forty-five homes on Inverness Ridge were destroyed and all Inverness residents were preparing to evacuate when fog settled over the peninsula on October 7, and the fire died. Inverness residents credited National Seashore Superintendent Don Neubacher with saving their homes, for he made the decision to deploy firefighters to protect homes before trying to save the park. They recognized that another super-intendent might have made a different decision, and all of Inverness would have burned.

When the damage was assessed, the fire had destroyed 12,354 acres, 15% of the National Seashore had burned, and $7 million had been spent fighting the blaze. Thankfully, no one was killed or even seri-ously injured. Within a week, four teenage boys admitted to acci-dentally starting the blaze. On September 30, they had been camp-ing illegally and had built a campfire, also illegal. When they left their campsite, they doused it with water and covered it with dirt, not realizing that the embers were still smoldering. All it took was a gust of wind to fan the embers and ignite the fire. The Marin County District Attorney decided not to prosecute the teens, both because they admitted it and were remorseful, but also because, from a practical sense, others also camped there illegally, and it would have been difficult to prove that it was their fire that caused the devastating blaze. Today, the NPS utilizes the fire-damaged land as an unanticipated, but valuable, learning laboratory where visitors and researchers, alike, can observe nature regenerating and rebuild-ing itself.

Point Reyes National Seashore Today

Since 1981, the waters off Point Reyes have been protected by the Gulf of Farallons National Marine Sanctuary, 948 square nautical miles stretching from Bodega Bay to Bolinas. In 1989, Washington also authorized the 397-square mile Cordell Bank National Marine Sanctuary off the coast of Point Reyes, banning drilling and mineral exploration.

Despite these protective measures, oil tankers continue to journey along its coastline. Two collided in 1971 under the Golden Gate Bridge, dumping 800,000 gallons of oil, killing seabirds, and blackening beaches from Sausalito to Point Reyes. Again, in October 1984, a Puerto Rican tanker exploded off the Golden Gate. As it was being towed to sea, it broke in two. The bow was towed to Richmond, but the stern, containing 1.5 million gallons of oil, sank in 2400 feet of water just off Half Moon Bay. Seeping oil again killed thousands of water fowl and marine animals. These accidents clearly illustrate just how vulnerable Point Reyes' coastal waters remain.

Constantly seeking to protect more land, three laws have expanded park acreage to its current size of 70,187 acres, 21,649 acres of which are leased for dairying or beef ranching. Today, Point Reyes National Seashore welcomes visitors who roam its hills, swim at its wonderful beaches, and enjoy unmatched ocean vistas. Many stop at the Park Headquarters at Bear Valley Ranch, wander around the lovely restored Pierce Point Ranch, walk down to the lighthouse, and explore the Drakes Beach Lifeboat Station. Most visit Kule Loklo (meaning "bear valley"), the replica Coast Miwok village, and some are even lucky enough to observe a celebration there.

At the end of the day, they enjoy the solitude of one of the many hike-in campsites, luxuriate at a wonderful inn, or stay at the National Seashore Hostel, the former Laguna Ranch. While wandering this magnificent peninsula, gazing at its lovely dairies, and exploring its small towns, it is easy to imagine Oscar, Julia, or Leland striding over this land they so loved.

108

Index

A

Carlisle Abbott 41, 72-73

B

Bear Valley 23, 35, 48, 55, 60, 89, 91, 102, 108
James Berry 24-26, 28, 47
Joseph Bien 67
Bolinas 5, 14, 20-22, 47, 55, 64, 74, 78- 81, 83-85, 88, 105- 108
Gregorio Briones 23
Dr. Galen Burdell 50

C

Juan Rodriguez Cabrillo 11
Sebastian Cermeno 17, 63
Coast Miwok 6-10, 19, 21, 39, 44, 108
Eugene Compton 92

D

Leonard David 61, 94, 97
Francis Drake 6, 11-17, 66, 88

E

E Antoni 85-86
Earthquake 5, 55, 57
Clair Engle 98, 100

F

Francis Fletcher 6-7, 13-14

G

Garcias 22-25, 27-29, 43, 48, 102

H

Hartwood 81-83
Dr. Edward Heims 96
Henrietta 82
Henry Bergh 88
Joseph Hetherington 27
Home Ranch 34, 36, 48, 93
Charles Webb Howard 31, 33, 45, 47-49, 53, 59-61, 74, 80-81, 87, 89

I

Inverness 5, 45, 54-58, 60, 83, 94, 96, 100, 102, 105-107

K

Isabel Kelly 7-10
John F. Kennedy 100-102

L

Colonel Jesse Langdon 91-92
Lifeboat Station 70, 79-82, 86- 88, 108
Life-Saving Station 72, 74-77, 79-80, 86, 90
Lighthouse 35, 63-68, 70-72, 74, 84, 86-88, 95, 108
Dewey Livingston 59, 66

M

MALT, 104
Guglielmo Marconi 77-79
Jack Mason 58, 94
Dr. Robert McMillan 27-28, 32
Mendozas 38, 80-81, 83, 85-86, 89-91, 98, 101
Mexican ranchos 7, 21-22, 29, 32
Clem Miller 98, 100, 102
missions 7, 18-19, 22
Munleon 84-85
Leland Stanford Murphy 53-55, 59, 92-95, 108

N

National Park Service 16, 41, 43, 59, 66, 72, 79, 81, 91, 94, 97-105, 107-108
National Seashore 5, 10, 23, 31, 36, 43, 48, 55, 70, 79, 94, 97-98, 100-103, 105-108
Nelsons 44, 95, 105

O

Olema 22, 24, 28-29, 43-44, 48, 50-51, 55, 58, 70-71, 95, 97, 101, 105-106
Jose Francisco Ortega 18-19
Antonio Maria Osio 25, 26

P

Bethuel Phelps 26
Pierce Ranch 41-43, 103, 108
Point Reyes Station 50, 56, 70, 75-76, 90, 95, 105-106
Gaspar de Portola 18-19

R

Radio Corporation of America 78-79, 95, 98
Railroad 33, 39, 47, 49-53, 59, 93, 105-106
Dr. Andrew Randall 26-28
Elbert Reeves 83-84
Richfield 83-84
rumrunners 59, 80, 93

S

Samoa 76-77
San Agustin 15-17
San Andreas Fault 5, 55
Shafters 29-34, 37-42, 47, 61, 65
   Emma 32-33, 48-49, 60-61, 89
   James 24, 31-34, 36, 43, 47-54,
   Julia 54-59, 92, 94, 98, 108
   Oscar 28, 31-34, 36-37, 47-49, 53, 59-61, 95, 108
Stephen Smith 25
Joseph Snook 25
Steele 39

U

Howard Underhill 80, 84
United Airlines DC-3 86-87

V

Sheriff G. N. Vischer 27
Vision Fire 106-107
Sebastian Vizcaino 17-18

W

Benjamin Winslow 43
World War II 31, 44, 79, 93-106

Sources

Although much of Point Reyes' fascinating history still resides in the memories of its long-time residents and resonates throughout the windswept peninsula, there is also a rich array of books documenting its stories. Hopefully, you have been inspired to continue your exploration of Point Reyes history. You may want to begin your journey with these books:

The Coast Miwok Indians of the Point Reyes Area by Sylvia Barker Thalman. National Park Service, 2001.

Discovering Francis Drake's California Harbor by Raymond Aker and Edward Von der Porten. Drake Navigators Guild, 2000.

Earthquake Bay: A History of Tomales Bay by Jack Mason. North Shore Books, 1976.

A Good Life: Dairy Farming in the Olema Valley by D. S. Livingston. National Park Service, 1995.

The History and Architecture of Point Reyes Lifeboat Station, Drakes Bay by D. S. Livingston and Steven Burke. National Park Service, 1991.

The History and Architecture of the Point Reyes Light Station by D. S. Livingston and Dave Snow. National Park Service, 1990.

History of Marin County, California by J. P. Munro-Fraser. Alley, Bowen & Co., 1880.

Interviews with Tom Smith and Maria Copa by Isabel Kelly. Compiled and edited by Mary T. Collier and Sylvia B. Thalman. Miwok Archeological Preserve of Marin, 1996.

Lost Harbor, The Controversy Over Drake's California Anchorage by Warren L. Hanna. University of California Press, 1979.

Point Reyes Historian (serial newsletter) by Jack Mason, editor. North Shore Books, 1976-1984.

Point Reyes, The Solemn Land by Jack Mason. North Shore Books, 1972.

Point Reyes West by Jack Mason. North Shore Books, 1981.

Ranching on the Point Reyes Peninsula. by D. S. Livingston. National Park Service, 1993.

Acknowledgments

Local historian Jack Mason left Point Reyes an invaluable legacy. He tirelessly interviewed its history-making characters; meticulously collected and protected precious letters, papers, and pictures; and wrote books and articles documenting the story that emerged. Upon his death, his Inverness home was donated to the Inverness Foundation, and his unique collection became the Jack Mason Museum of West Marin History. Few towns have had such a committed historian and the Point Reyes story is greatly enhanced as a result of his passion for this wonderful peninsula. This book would be far less rich without his writings.

In addition to Jack, Point Reyes is blessed with yet another committed historian, Dewey Livingston, also a resident of Inverness. As the National Park Historian, he compiled a treasure trove of information in his voluminous studies of the ranches, lighthouse, and lifesaving facilities. Clearly today's most prominent historian of the area, much of the information in this book was derived from his comprehensive publications.